Published by:

Pietas Publications
Waynesboro, Virginia, USA
web: www.jasperburns.com
email: pietas@jasperburns.com

WILT THE WINNER

SETTING THE RECORDS STRAIGHT

BY JASPER BURNS

COPYRIGHT 2019

To Randy Coulling, my next door neighbor, who played for the Old Dominion University basketball team in the early 1970s and is the only coach ever to win both the boys' and girls' high school state championships in the same school year (Waynesboro High School (Virginia), 1990-91).

WILT THE WINNER
By Jasper Burns
Contents

INTRODUCTION

In 1973, at the end of his illustrious NBA career, Wilt Chamberlain wrote his autobiography, entitled *Wilt: Just Like Any Other 7-Foot Black Millionaire Who Lives Next Door*. On page 20, he tells a story from his childhood, of visiting his uncle's farm in Laneview, Essex County, Virginia in about 1950 as a 6'11" high schooler.

The young Wilt was perplexed when the locals gawked at him, pointing and saying "Pickett Nelson, Pickett Nelson." He asked his uncle who or what Pickett Nelson was, and was told that a man by that name had lived in the area 20 or 30 years before who was eight or eight and a half feet tall. Supposedly, Mr. Nelson just vanished one day and was never seen again. Wilt's uncle told him that his height reminded people of Pickett Nelson.

Wilt wrote: "It was a great story, I thought, and I always wondered if the old guy made it up so I wouldn't feel self-conscious about those people pointing at me, or if there really had been a Pickett Nelson and just how tall he really was."

Wilt didn't have access to the internet in 1973, so he had no easy way of discovering that Pickett Nelson was a real person. To quote from the January 20, 1892 issue of the Pittsburgh (PA) Dispatch:

THE TALLEST MAN IS DEAD. Colonel Pickett Nelson Succumbs at Baltimore to Typhoid Fever.

BALTIMORE, Jan. 19. – [Special] - "Colonel" Pickett Nelson, who claimed to be "the tallest man on earth," died here to-day. He had been ill for three weeks with typhoid fever. His body measures eight feet five inches in length. In life he claimed to be eight feet one inch tall and to weigh 387 pounds. After his death his frame relaxed and became four inches longer than it had been. Nelson is a colored man and was born in 1861 in Essex county, Va....

The point? Sometimes legends are real. Sometimes they grow in stature with time, sometimes they diminish, and sometimes they are remembered with accuracy. All three of these have happened to the legend of Wilt Chamberlain.

As someone who grew up "gawking and pointing" at the greatest athlete I have ever seen, I want to pay my respects to "The Dipper" by offering some counter arguments to those who have tried to tarnish his legend – through jealousy, animosity, or ignorance - while he was alive and since he passed away by labelling him "selfish" and "a loser" or an artifact of his era. It irks me that the legend of Wilt Chamberlain, which should be second to none, is diminished by lies and misunderstandings.

I started watching Wilt on black and white television in about 1963 or 1964, when I was 11 or 12. He seemed like a mythological figure to me – like Achilles or Paul Bunyan or Little John of Robin Hood fame. I was mesmerized by the grace, power, and efficiency of his movements on the court. He was always under control, and generally *in* control of whatever was happening close to the basket on both ends of the court. For the rest of his career, I followed his success in the sports pages and on television.

Wilt played as if he took the old motto seriously: "It's not whether you win or lose; it's how you play the game." He had incredible physical and emotional composure – never fouling out of a single game during his entire 1205 game professional career (though he was ejected twice by the referees on technical fouls). He was rarely involved in fights with other players, though he was probably subjected to more physical abuse and hard fouls than any other player in history.

Some other players with "winner" reputations seemed to prefer Vince Lombardi's maxim: "Winning isn't everything; it's the only thing." Michael Jordan's push-off on Byron Russell that set up the shot that won his sixth championship is well-known - and admired by most as symbolic of his relentless competitive spirit. This sort of thing was definitely not Wilt's style. He played fair and square, which some see as a weakness in his game. I don't.

I gained some insight into how Wilt played basketball when I played with young children as an adult. I had to move a certain way and remain under control to avoid hurting the kids.

Wilt was like a man among boys because of his incredible strength, leaping ability, and coordination - but not so much his height. Contrary to popular belief, the average NBA center was as tall during his career as he is today (see Chapter 4). It seemed that Wilt didn't want to take "unfair" advantage of his less-gifted opponents, so he challenged himself to play an all-around game. Winning wasn't "the only thing" to him – playing with dignity and fairness and unparalleled skill was.

As a boy, I wasn't all that concerned that Wilt's team usually lost to the Boston Celtics – *everybody* lost to the Boston Celtics. They were a well-oiled machine that knew how to win because they had great players, a great coach – and because they had been doing it together for so long. But Wilt was always the most spectacular player on the court and I was always thrilled by his play. It never occurred to me that the losses reflected on him personally because he was almost always absolutely brilliant. It wasn't his fault that the Celtics were a better team than his.

In his 14 year career, Wilt missed the playoffs only once. He won 2 championships, competed in 6 finals and in 12 conference finals (losing 6 times to the eventual champion). As will be argued in Chapter 3, this makes him the most successful superstar in NBA playoff history other than Magic Johnson (who played with a man named Kareem Abdul-Jabbar) and some of the players on Bill Russell's Boston Celtics team.

Perhaps now, almost 20 years since his passing, it is time to look at Wilt's career from the vantage point of history. When he retired in 1973, the NBA was only 27 years old. Now it is more than 72 years old. We have seen too many things to buy into the old saw that Wilt "should have won" a parcel of championships simply because he was so big and talented. For example:

In the years since Wilt retired, we have seen Kareem Abdul-Jabbar, after winning a ring with Milwaukee at the age of 23, play for the next 8 years (1971-72 through 1978-79) – the prime of his career (ages 24-31) – without earning a ring and only making the conference finals twice and the finals once. It is entirely possible that, without the advent of Magic Johnson in 1979-80, he might have ended his magnificent 20 year career with only one championship.

We have seen Michael Jordan tear up the league for the first six years of his career without ever winning as much as a conference final, much less a ring. In fact, his playoff W-L record for the first three years of his career was 1-9.

We have also seen Lebron James – perhaps the closest parallel to Wilt in subsequent history – play superbly against the Golden State Warriors in four straight championship series (2015-2018) and walk away with a record of 1 and 3. Does that make him a "loser" or "owned" by Steph Curry, or Kevin Durant, or Draymond Green as Wilt was said to have been "owned" by the Celtics' Bill Russell?

Perhaps Kareem, Jordan, and Lebron – and numerous other supremely talented players who came up short or even missed the playoffs altogether – have proved what Wilt could not during his career: that no one player can win a championship all by himself. Perhaps we have finally outgrown the "winners and losers" style of sports coverage that prevailed during Wilt's day.

Or have we? I am constantly seeing ridiculous claims about Wilt – that he lost because he choked in big games and only cared about stats, that he was a terrible teammate, that he didn't play defense, that he couldn't do anything but dunk, etc., etc. And most of this rubbish comes from people who never even saw him play in real time and can't possibly have seen more than 2 or 3 per cent of his career on video (because that is all that survives).

Some have even claimed that Wilt would be a benchwarmer today. To suggest that a highly intelligent, fundamentally sound, marathon-running, supremely coordinated, 7 foot 3 inch (with today's shoes), 290 pound player who could run 40 yards in 4.4

seconds, had a 45+ inch vertical, and could bench press more than 500 pounds would be anything but a superstar in any era is the height of stupidity. It is also an insult to history and to every player who played against Wilt Chamberlain, from Bob Cousy to Kareem Abdul-Jabbar.

The purpose of this book is not to argue that Wilt was the GOAT – the Greatest of All Time – or that he was better than Russell or Shaq or Kareem or Jordan or Lebron or whoever. Trying to name the best of anything as complex as a basketball player is, in my opinion, a childish exercise. (More about that later.) Rather, I hope to pay homage to one of my boyhood heroes, and perhaps to loosen some of the barnacles of blame that have attached themselves to the legend of Wilt Chamberlain.

1. CAREER SKETCH

Wilt's career divides into three discreet phases: 1) The young phenom who could score from inside or outside and who set scoring and rebounding records that have never been approached; 2) the playmaker/scorer/rebounder who led the league in assists and dominated play in the paint at both ends of the court; 3) the defensive stopper, who rarely shot the ball but seldom missed when he did and led his team to unprecedented success (69 wins in a season, 33 wins in a row, and a Los Angeles Laker's championship).

In high school, Wilt received an unprecedented amount of attention – from colleges hoping to recruit him to the national media. His Overbrook High School Panthers lost a total of 3 games in 3 years and won two all-city (Philadelphia) and three all-public school championships, losing one all-city title when Wilt was quadruple-teamed. Wilt also led his local YMCA team to the national championship.

Chamberlain attended the University of Kansas from 1955-58. At the time, freshman were not allowed to play with the varsity, but Wilt began his Jayhawk career by leading the freshmen to victory over the highly-touted varsity squad in an exhibition game, scoring 42 points and grabbing 29 rebounds.

As a sophomore and junior, Wilt played superbly, but was frustrated by the defensive tactics that were used against him, including physical abuse, double, triple, and quadruple teaming, and – in the days before the shot clock – stalling by holding the ball. This last strategy was used in the 1956-57 NCAA finals when Kansas lost to the North Carolina Tarheels (coached by Frank Maguire, who would be Wilt's favorite professional coach) by a score of 54-53 in three overtimes.

Wilt was so fed up with what he was subjected to in college that he passed up his senior year, explaining his decision in a *Look Magazine* article entitled *"Why I Am Leaving College."* Kansas' record for his two years on the varsity was 42-8 and Wilt averaged 30 points and 18 rebounds for his college career.

Wilt said that his favorite basketball experience was his tenure with the Harlem Globetrotters, which began in 1958 and continued for almost a decade during the off-seasons after he joined the NBA in 1959. He enjoyed the team atmosphere with the Globies, the international travel, and the opportunity to display his talents and win a lot of games without the pressure and harassment that he received elsewhere.

But Wilt wanted to prove himself against the best players in the world, so he joined his college class in moving to the NBA in 1959, playing for his hometown Philadelphia Warriors.

In his first year, he took a team that had a record of 32-40 and missed the playoffs the year before to 49-26 and a loss in six games in the Division finals to the reigning champion Boston Celtics. Wilt broke the all-time NBA regular season scoring and rebounding records in his first year, averaging 37.6 and 27.0, and won the MVP and Rookie of the Year awards. Not bad for a rookie season.

Wilt continue to set numerous scoring and rebounding records for the next few years, following the Warriors to San Francisco in 1962 and then being traded back to Philadelphia in 1965 where the Syracuse team had moved and been renamed the 76ers.

Chamberlain's game changed with the 76ers. He curtailed his scoring and became more of a distributor, finishing 3rd in the league in assists in 1966-67 and leading the league in total assists in 1967-68 – unheard of before or since from the center position. Wilt's team won the NBA championship in 1967, putting an end to the Boston Celtics' streak of 8 straight titles.

Boston bounced back the following year (1967-68), and Wilt was traded after the season ended to the Los Angeles Lakers, where he joined superstars Jerry West and Elgin Baylor. The Lakers lost to the Celtics in the 1969 Finals, after which Wilt's friend and rival Bill Russell retired.

After only 12 games in 1969, Wilt blew out his knee,

rupturing his patellar ligament. After surgery and Herculean rehabilitation efforts, Wilt defied all predictions and returned to the Lakers in time for the playoffs.

In the finals, they faced the New York Knicks, led by Willis Reed and Walt "Clyde" Frazier. The Knicks played better team ball than the Lakers, who had been without Chamberlain for most of the season. In the 7th game of the series, the injured Willis Reed (who had missed game 6) limped onto the floor and inspired his team by hitting his first two baskets. The Knicks went on to win behind Frazier's 36 points and 19 assists.

It always galled me that a great deal was made about Reed's courageous return to action in game 7, but virtually nothing was said about Wilt's even more courageous return after what could have been a career-ending injury.

After his surgery, Wilt had less lateral mobility than before. However, he was still a formidable rebounder and shot blocker, and he was still capable of big-time scoring, as he proved in game 6 of the Knicks series when he scored 45 points on 20 of 27 shooting.

The following year, the Lakers entered the playoffs without either Jerry West or Elgin Baylor, both sidelined by injuries. When Wilt's undermanned Lakers fell to Abdul-Jabbar's Milwaukee Bucks in the 1971 Western Conference finals, the Milwaukee fans gave Wilt a standing ovation in recognition of his heroics against Kareem – something unimaginable when Wilt was the designated NBA boogie man. Wilt generally played very well against Kareem, often blocking his shots including the vaunted sky-hook, even though he was almost 11 years older and less mobile post-surgery.

Wilt also received much praise and even affection a year later when he led the Lakers to their first championship with a brilliant final game performance (24 points, 29 rebounds, 4 assists, and 6 blocks), despite playing with one broken hand and the other one sprained. The Lakers had set records that year for most wins (69) and longest winning streak (33 Games).

The Lakers lost the 1972-73 finals to the New York Knicks, but Wilt set a regular season record that year for field goal percentage (72.7%) and led the league in rebounding for the 11th time.

In 1973, at the age of 37, Wilt jumped to the rival league, the American Basketball Association (ABA), and signed a contract to play for the San Diego Conquistadors. However, the Lakers' owner Jack Kent Cooke showed that he was more a businessman than a basketball fan by asserting his legal rights under Wilt's contract to prohibit from playing for any team other than the Lakers. Wilt coached in San Diego for one year instead, and then left professional basketball (aside from occasional appearances with the Globetrotters) for good.

Late in his career, Wilt had finally begun to get the fan appreciation he deserved. This was partly because times had changed and his lifestyle and individuality were more acceptable. It was also partly because he was no longer the scariest player in the league – that dubious honor had been passed to Kareem Abdul-Jabbar.

After retirement, Wilt stayed in top physical condition until near the end of his life. He embarked on a professional volleyball career, which lasted even longer than his NBA career, and ran marathons into his late fifties, maintaining a weight of 275 – 25 to 35 pounds below his final NBA playing weight.

Many times during his forties and even fifties, various NBA teams seriously pursued the idea of bringing Chamberlain back into the league, but it never happened. Wilt loved his lifestyle and freedom after basketball. Sportswriter Frank Deford once wrote:

> *I'm not sure there's ever been a star athlete other than Wilt who was so uncomfortable when playing and so much happier retired.*

Coach Larry Brown told a remarkable story about Wilt's continuing ability to dominate a basketball court against top

NBA talent many years after his retirement:

> *I'll tell you a great Magic [Johnson] story. Um, I'm the coach at UCLA and he used to come to the men's gym and organize games... And he used to make the sides and stack them, so one night I'm watching ... in the stands. Wilt Chamberlain's playing with four of my freshmen against Magic, Bernard King, James Worthy, Byron Scott, and, uh, [A. C.] Green.*
>
> *And it's game point. Magic throws a sky hook and Wilt blocks it. Magic calls "game"' And Wilt says "That wasn't goaltending; that was a clean block." And Magic took the ball and said "Game over. Next."*
>
> *And Wilt said "Hey Coach, was that goaltending?" And I said "No. That was a clean block"' Magic said "What do you think he's going to say – they're his kids!"*
>
> *And Wilt says "All right. Look. We're going to play a game till 12, winner stays, and there will be no more shots made at this basket." He blocked every shot. Forty-three years old. He was blocking everything. It was unbelievable.*

The interviewer interjected:

> *Somebody who used to play in those 80s games who I asked "Who's the best player you ever played with or against?" told me it was about a 50 year old Wilt Chamberlain at those UCLA pick-up games. He was that kind of physical presence.*

Now, Larry Brown said that Wilt was 43 at the time this happened, which would place the game in 1979 or 1980. However, the players he mentioned on Magic's team (other than Bernard King) weren't Lakers before 1985-86 and were unlikely to have been present, meaning that Wilt was probably in his latest 40's or even as much as 50 years old at the time. And he was playing against a super team – Magic, Worthy, King, and Green were All-Stars and Byron Scott was no slouch (lifetime

14.1 ppg on 48% shooting in 14 years).

Wilt's health declined rapidly as he entered his 60s. Battling heart trouble, diabetes, and in need of a hip replacement, he passed away on October 12, 1999 at the age of 63.

2. INDIVIDUAL SUCCESS

As so little film footage survives from Wilt's career, we have to rely on the written record, the memories of those who saw him play, and on his statistics. However, when comparing stats from one era to another, the numbers should be accompanied by a flurry of asterisks. They simply can't be compared in an apples to apples kind of way. Conditions are always changing.

For example, these factors can inflate or deflate a player's numbers: pace of the game (affecting potential number of points, rebounds, assists, etc.); number of teams (how recent expansion affected talent level); minutes played per player per game; rules of the game (and how they affect how statistics are reported and how players can operate); balance of a player's team (a high scorer on a weak team may not be better than a moderate scorer on a strong team); and so on and so on.

The truth is, there is no completely fair way to use statistics to compare players *within* an era, not to mention between eras. Nevertheless, comparative statistics for a given year may be useful to some extent. The scoring, rebounding, assist, shot-blocking, and steals champions are likely to be among the best – if not the best – in that category for that particular year. And the larger the margin between them and their rivals, the more likely that their supremacy in that category is for real.

Accordingly, if we look at Wilt's rank among his contemporaries in the performance categories for which records survive, we can get some idea of his dominance. Rather than trying to match absolute numbers of points, rebounds, and assists, I compared Wilt's record to those of other superstars by awarding points for leading the league or coming in second or third (unfortunately, no official records were kept for blocked shots or steals during Wilt's time).

I awarded 1 point for a third place finish in one of these three categories, 2 points for second place, and 3 points for first place, and then I divided the total number of career points by each player's years of eligibility (i. e. years with sufficient games played for ranking). (Note: I've taken away Wilt's 1967 assist title and given him second place because he actually had the second highest per game average. Total assists rather than per game average was the official criterion at that time.) Here are the results for some of the most famous names in basketball:

Wilt – 4.69
Oscar Robertson – 2.57
Michael Jordan – 2.38
Bill Russell – 2.08
Magic Johnson – 2.00
Jerry West – 1.46
Shaquille O'Neal – 1.41
Kareem Abdul-Jabbar – 1.15
Lebron James – 1.13
Kobe Bryant – 0.89
Elgin Baylor – 0.67
Larry Bird – 0.25

This means that in an average year, Wilt was first in one category (3 points) and at least third (1 point) but closer to second (2 points) in another category. No other player even averaged a single first place for each year of his career.

But let's take a closer look at some of the categories in which Wilt excelled.

SCORING

Certainly the most dazzling of Wilt Chamberlain's statistical accomplishments are his scoring records: 100 points in a single game; 4,029 points in one regular season; 50.4 points per game for a full regular season (1961-1962); seven consecutive scoring titles; 118 games with 50 points or more; 32 games with 60 points or more; 6 games with 70 or more points; a career scoring average of 30.1 (only 0.05 below Michael Jordan's all-time record) - even though Wilt intentionally and dramatically curtailed his scoring for the last *seven years of his fourteen year career.*

During the first part of his career, when he was leading the league in scoring, Chamberlain went out of his way to take difficult shots. He shot finger rolls, hook shots, bank shots, fade-away jumpers and the like rather than muscle his way to the basket and jam the ball through the hoop, which he could have done a lot more often than he did. This was partly to avoid offensive fouls and partly to demonstrate the range of his offensive skills. A former member of the Harlem Globetrotters, Wilt understood that NBA basketball was entertainment as well as competition. He took pride in the full range of his abilities and knew that paying customers wanted to see them displayed.

It has been pointed out that much of Wilt's scoring occurred early in his career when the pace of the game was fast and scores were higher than in later years. This is certainly true, but it doesn't change the fact that Wilt was overwhelmingly the highest scorer in the NBA. Consider the following scoring averages with the margins of victory over the second best scorer in the league for each of Wilt's early "high-scoring" years:

> 1959-60: 37.6 ppg, 6.4 ppg over number 2
> 1960-61: 38.4 ppg, 4.4 ppg over number 2
> 1961-62: 50.4 ppg, 18.8 ppg over number 2
> 1962-63: 44.8 ppg, 10.8 ppg over number 2
> 1963-64: 36.9 ppg, 5.5 ppg over number 2
> 1964-65: 34.7 ppg, 3.7 ppg over number 2
> 1965-66: 33.5 ppg, 2.2 ppg over number 2

One of the many false charges made against Wilt during his playing days was that, later in his career, his scoring numbers dropped because he was no longer capable of putting up big numbers. For the first three years after the change in his style of play, Wilt responded to these comments with isolated big scoring games to prove otherwise. For example, note his high scoring game for the following low-scoring years:

> 1966-67: 24.1 ppg, high game 58 points
> 1967-68: 24.3 ppg, high game 68 points
> 1968-69: 20.5 ppg, high game 66 points
> 1969-70: 27.3 ppg, high game 43 points
> 1970-71: 20.7 ppg, high game 41 points
> 1971-72: 14.8 ppg, high game 32 points
> 1972-73: 13.2 ppg, high game 29 points

In 1997, two years before he died, Wilt was interviewed with Bill Russell by Ahmad Rashad.:

Ahmad Rashad: If you were playing today, how many points would you average?

Wilt: At [age] 30, I could probably average 60 or 70. And I'm saying that politely. I'm not trying to dismantle your belief on how great the athlete of today is, but the game would best suit me. Believe me; it would best suit me.

That same year, when he and Russell were interviewed by Bob Costas, he explained his thinking more fully:

Bob Costas: What would you do today?... You're 25, 25 years old, the 25 year old Wilt Chamberlain, who didn't just have the inside game, who had the fade-away, could put the ball on the floor a bit... The 25 year old Wilt Chamberlain transplanted into today's NBA. What do you do?

Wilt: It's simple for me... You see, with the new rules, which are all slanted to help the offense, now, when I get the ball, instead of having two and three people and Russ all at me at the same time, I'm by myself with one guy. I would love it. I would love it. Fifty points. Maybe 60 points. Maybe 70 points a game.

The former New York Knick great Walt "Clyde" Frazier, who played against Wilt in three NBA final series, added his two cents worth in a 2010 interview:

Chamberlain averaged 50 points a game; he'd probably average 75 a game if he were playing today. You know why I say that? Because you can't put your hand on guys. When I played you could hand check them. Now you can't hand check them. So it's much more difficult to stop players that way.

Wilt's claims in 1997 seemed outlandish at a time when the average NBA *team* was only scoring about 96 points a game. But Wilt's numbers may not have been so unreasonable. If the question was rephrased this way: "Given the pace of the game in the early 1960s, when the average team scored about 119 points per game, your mandate to score as much as you could, and with the modern rules that favor the offensive player, how many points per game would you average?"

The truth is that no one could have kept Wilt out of the modern "no charge" zone under the basket – especially without hand checking – and no one could have stopped him from scoring once he was in it.

It should be remembered that, near the end of 1962, Wilt had consecutive games of 67, 65, 61, 100, and 58 points, for an average of 70 points a game. If depending on one player to do so much scoring seems like a bad strategy, consider that in that year, when Wilt averaged 50.4 points per game for the entire regular season, his team lost to the reigning and soon-to-repeat champion Boston Celtics in the 7th game of the conference finals - by a single basket.

FIELD GOAL PERCENTAGE

When his high scoring average was cited by Wilt's detractors as proof of his selfishness, he pointed out that it made sense for the player who made the highest percentage of shots on his team him to shoot most often. To support his point, Wilt's shooting percentages compared to the cumulative averages for his teammates through the 1965-66 season are listed below. One has to wonder how it would have affected their won-loss record if Wilt had been shy about scoring:

1959-60:	Team fg% = 39.0	Wilt's fg% = 46.1
1960-61:	Team fg% = 39.2	Wilt's fg% = 50.9
1961-62:	Team fg% = 40.2	Wilt's fg% = 50.6
1962-63:	Team fg% = 41.2	Wilt's fg% = 52.8
1963-64:	Team fg% = 40.2	Wilt's fg% = 52.4
1964-65:	Teams fg% = 39.8	Wilt's fg% = 51.0
1965-66:	Team fg% = 41.6	Wilt's fg% = 54.0

Chamberlain was the first player in NBA history to make more than half of his shots for an entire season, the first to make more than 60% of his shots, and the first to make more than 70% of his shots. His teams enjoyed great success when his coaches asked him to fire away, though they were even more successful later in his career when he was surrounded by good enough shooters to use a more balanced attack.

Wilt's lifetime field goal percentage is 54% (52.2% in the playoffs) - excellent by the standards of any era, but these numbers should be considered in the context of his time. They reflect a very different style of play in the NBA when it was run and gun, with high-scoring games and generally low shooting percentages. Interior defense was tough and charging fouls often called, so most players settled for mid-range and long-range jump shots, set shots, or hook shots. Prolific jump shooter Jack Twyman lead the league with 45.2% in 1958, two years before Wilt arrived in the NBA.

Wilt led the league in field goal percentage 9 times in 13 seasons of eligibility while averaging 22.5 field goal attempts per game for his career. In 1967, Wilt set the all-time record by making 35 shots in a row over 4 games. He also had games in which he was 18 for 18, 16 for 16, 15 for 15, and 14 for 14.

In his final year, he set a mark which still stands 45 years later as the all-time record: 72.7% while averaging 13.2 points on 7.1 shots per game.

Chamberlain's regular season field goal percentages by year are given below with his regular season ranking:

1959-60 - 46.1% - (6th in league)
1960-61 - 50.9% - (1st in league)
1961-62 - 50.6% - (2nd in league)
1962-63 - 52.8% - (1st in league)
1963-64 - 52.4% - (2nd in league)
1964-65 - 51.0% - (1st in league)
1965-66 – 54.0% - (1st in league)
1966-67 – 68.3% - (1st in league)
1967-68 – 59.5% - (1st in league)
1968-69 – 58.3% - (1st in league)
1969-70 – 56.8% - (played only 12 games)
1970-71 – 54.5% - (3rd in league)
1971-72 – 64.9% - (1st in league)
1972-73 – 72.7% - (1st in league)

Wilt is the all-time rebounding leader in the NBA, both in terms of total rebounds and rebounds per game. He also set the single game (55), season (1960-61 - 2,149 rebounds, or 27.2 rpg), and career (23,924 rebounds, 22.9 rpg) records. However, as with scoring, his actual numbers should be considered in context because of the changing pace of the NBA game and the resulting changes in available rebounds.

What matters is that Wilt led the league 11 times in his 13 years of eligibility (he only played 12 regular season games in 1970 and did not qualify for the title). Bill Russell was the leader in 1963-64 and 1964-65, with Wilt coming in a close second.

Wilt improved on his regular season career average of 22.9 rebounds per game in the playoffs, averaging 24.5 rebounds in 13 years while leading the league 8 times.

Bill Russell and Dennis Rodman are the only two players who can reasonably be compared to Wilt in this category. Wilt said that Russell was better because he had a higher career average per game for the playoffs than Wilt did (24.9). However, as with scoring, Wilt's playoff rebounding average is depressed by the fact that most of his playoff games occurred later in his career, by which time the game had slowed down and fewer rebounds were available.

Rodman was a phenomenal rebounder, leading the league 7 times (career average 13.1 per game) and posting a higher percentage of total team rebounds than either Wilt or Bill. Of course, Rodman was not an integral part of his teams' offense, being neither a scorer nor a playmaker, so he was able to concentrate on offensive rebounding, at which he excelled, averaging 4.8 per game for his career. (Offensive rebounds were not recorded separately in Wilt's day.)

It has often been pointed out that Rodman accomplished his feats despite the fact that he was "only" six foot seven. However, Bill Russell once noted that the vast majority of rebounds are grabbed at chest height or below, so that a player's height is not really as relevant as it might seem. This is borne out by the fact that many stellar rebounders have been even shorter than Rodman (e.g. Elgin Baylor (6'5"), Oscar Robertson (6'5"), Charles Barkley (6'5"), Wes Unseld (6'6"), Russell Westbrook (6'3")).

Wilt's rebounding stats are given below, with his rank in the league indicated. To show his dominance in this category irrespective of absolute numbers, the number of rebounds per game that Wilt averaged more than his closest rival <u>not named Bill Russell</u> is also indicated for each year:

1959-60 – 27.0 - (1st) +10.0 (Bob Pettit)
1960-61 – 27.2 - (1st) +6.9 (Bob Pettit)
1961-62 – 25.6 – (1st) +6.6 (Walt Bellamy)
1962-63 – 24.3 - (1st) +7.9 (Walt Bellamy)
1963-64 – 22.3 - (2nd to Bill Russell) +4.9 (Jerry Lucas)
1964-65 – 22.9 - (2nd to Bill Russell) +2.9 (Jerry Lucas)
1965-66 – 24.6 - (1st) +3.5 (Jerry Lucas)
1966-67 – 24.2 - (1st) +2.9 (Nate Thurmond)
1967-68 – 23.8 - (1st) +4.8 (Jerry Lucas)
1968-69 – 21.1 - (1st) +1.4 (Nate Thurmond)
1969-70 – 18.4 - (played 12 games, Elvin Hayes 1st with 16.9)
1970-71 – 18.2 - (1st) +1.3 (Wes Unseld)
1971-72 – 19.2 - (1st) +1.6 (Wes Unseld)
1972-73 – 18.6 - (1st) +1.5 (Nate Thurmond)

Philadelphia 76er's statistician Harvey Pollack remembered the record 55 rebound performance better than Wilt did.

> *When the NBA had a big anniversary party in New York, [Wilt] called the NBA and requested that I be invited. That resulted in me being in a hotel room with George Mikan, Julius Erving, Bill Russell and Wilt. My only regret in life is that I didn't have a tape machine to record all the stories that were told about their NBA careers.*

> *Wilt was the butt of one of Russell's stories. I just sat there and listened. Finally I asked if I could tell one anecdote. They all agreed. So I said, "Wilt do you remember who you posted your 55 rebounds against?" Wilt said, "I think it was*

against New York."

"Wrong Wilt, it was Russell," I said.

Wilt exploded from his seat and stood up and pointed at Russell's face and yelled, "Now I remember it was you," and everybody in the room roared in laughter.

(from The Greatest, *by Harvey Pollack, NBA Encyclopedia, Playoff Edition, 2006)*

ASSISTS

My most vivid memories of watching Wilt play are from his Philadelphia 76ers days – especially 1966-67 and 1967-68 when he was the fulcrum of the offense and the bulwark of the defense. For those two seasons, Wilt averaged 24 points on better than 60% shooting, 24 rebounds, 8 assists, and (unofficially) at least 8-10 blocked shots per game.

There were only 10 teams in the NBA in 1966-67 and 12 in 1967-68 and the talent level was high. Wilt's team was loaded, with forwards Luke Jackson, Billy Cunningham, and Chet Walker and guards Hal Greer, Wally (later Wali) Jones, and Larry Costello. The 76ers set a record in 1967 with 68 wins against 13 losses in the regular season and won the championship, but "fell" to a still-impressive 62-20 the following year and lost the title in 1968 because of injuries and the resurgent Boston Celtics.

What I see with my mind's eye is Wilt setting up on offense to the left of the key, holding the ball high above his head, his arm swooping and craning as his teammates swirled around him, using Wilt's body to screen off their man and cutting to the basket. Wilt either dropped the ball or threw a bounce pass behind him for a layup or he found the open man for a jumper. Or, if the defense was too tight, he would turn and wheel in for a dunk or finger roll, or fall away for a bank shot from 10-15 feet.

On the other end of the court, Wilt was the most effective rim protector ever, blocking or altering shot after shot and scooping up rebounds at his usual league-leading rate.

The Sixers were a machine – undoubtedly the best team in the NBA - and Wilt was their engine. The 1966-67 76ers are still cited as among the best teams in NBA history – Wilt considered it the best he ever played for.

It was this style of play that allowed Wilt to become the most successful playmaking center in NBA history, finishing the regular season as the number 3 assist maker in 1966-67 and leading the league in total assists (second in average per game) in 1967-68.

Much has been made of the fact that Wilt made the assist title a goal before the 1967-68 season, implying that this was the only reason he became a passer, to embellish his record book. But this was the style of play chosen by Coach Hannum, and if Wilt's personal goals helped him fulfill his role for the team, then why not?

On the other hand, it is true that Wilt chided Chet Walker, the third leading scorer behind Wilt and Hal Greer, because of his habit of taking an unnecessary dribble before shooting a wide open shot. Under the rules of the day, the passer was deprived of an assist if the shooter dribbled before shooting.

(This is no longer true today. The "dribble" rule and other guidelines were changed and assists are much now more easily acquired. This should be taken into consideration when comparing stats between eras.)

In a recent interview, Phil Jackson derided Wilt for stalling the offense early in his career by refusing to pass up-court. To quote:

> *[Wilt] used to take his time [getting down court on offense]. In fact, when he rebounded a lot of times he'd make the guards come back to him to get the ball so he'd be down when the ball got to the other end of the court. One of the things coach [Bill] Sharman did...when he got Wilt, he*

got Wilt to outlet the ball to Goody [Gail Goodrich] and to [Jerry] West...

What Phil neglected to point out, however, was that during the first two phases of Wilt's career – his high scoring days and subsequent role on the 76ers as a distributor – his team's offensive strategy depended on his being present on the offensive end - for scoring, passing, and rebounding.

In my recollection, Wilt never hesitated to move the ball down court quickly if his team had numbers on a fast break. Otherwise, however, he was needed as the first scoring option or, later, as the playmaker. This changed under Bill Sharman when Wilt's principal role became defensive stopper on a fast-breaking team rather than scorer or assist man.

Wilt's yearly assist averages and totals (with rank in the league if in the top 20):

> 1959-60 – 168 assists – 2.3 per game
> 1960-61 – 148 assists – 1.9 per game
> 1961-62 – 192 assists – 2.4 per game
> 1962-63 – 275 assists (16) – 3.4 per game (15)
> 1963-64 – 403 assists (4) – 5.0 per game (6)
> 1964-65 – 250 assists (16) – 3.4 per game (12)
> 1965-66 – 414 assists (7) – 5.2 per game (7)
> 1966-67 – 630 assists (3) – 7.8 per game (3)
> 1967-68 – 702 assists (1) – 8.6 per game (2)
> 1968-69 – 366 assists (20) – 4.5 per game (19)
> 1969-70 – 49 assists – 4.1 per game
> 1970-71 – 352 assists – 4.3 per game
> 1971-72 – 329 assists – 4.0 per game
> 1972-73 – 365 assists – 4.5 per game

DEFENSE AND BLOCKED SHOTS

Defense is as important to a basketball team's success as offense, so it is unfortunate that there are fewer individual statistics that unequivocally demonstrate an individual player's defensive value. Sophisticated modern record-keeping can monitor this to some degree, though there are still variables that are difficult to assess (e.g. team defense vs. individual defense).

In Wilt's day, no official records were kept for basic stats such as blocked shots and steals. Rebounds are another important indicator of defensive effectiveness, and we have seen how Wilt excelled in that area. But there are few hard facts that demonstrate what a defensive force he was.

Phil Jackson has made the claim that Wilt didn't play defense with 5 fouls. Again, this certainly doesn't agree with my recollections, nor with the documentation. Wilt only had 5 fouls 30 times in his entire 1205 game career, including 13 times in 160 playoff games. (Incidentally, Phil Jackson was only present as a player on two of those occasions and Wilt's team won both games.)

I do remember a couple of must win playoff games when Wilt had 5 fouls:

In 1965, he picked up his 5th foul against Boston in the 6th game of the conference finals. The Celtics immediately took it to him in an effort to get him out of this must-win game for Philadelphia. Rather than play it safe, Wilt responded by blocking consecutive shots by Bill Russell and Tommy Heinsohn.

In Overtime of the 4th game of the 1972 finals against the New York Knicks, Wilt blocked two shots and played fierce defense despite having 5 fouls.

However, I wouldn't have blamed him if he did let up on defense when in foul trouble. His overall value to his team was so high that this would have been the smart thing to do, unless it was absolute do-or-die crunch time, as in that Celtics game. Wilt knew his value as defender, rebounder, scorer, and passer – he wasn't about to go out on cheap fouls.

Regarding blocked shots, it is reported that Harvey Pollack, who was known as "Super Stat," kept some records on the side.

In addition to regular game statistics, he kept unofficial records of blocked shots, steals, and other game details.

Pollack recorded a "quadruple-double" game in which Wilt had double digits in points, rebounds, blocks, and assists as well as a "quintuple-double" game in which he added double digits in steals.

Various news sources recorded Wilt's blocked shot statistics for 112 games. These unofficial numbers are included in the game logs at the back of this book. Wilt's average for those 112 games, extending from 1959 to 1973, was 8.8 blocks per game, which should be compared to Mark Eaton's all-time NBA single season record of 5.6. And these sources did not cherry-pick which games to record; games with as few as 1-3 blocks are included.

Wilt was often criticized for his occasional habit of swatting shots out of bounds rather than tipping them to teammates, thus returning possession to his opponents. This is probably a fair criticism. However, it is difficult to measure the psychologically intimidating impact of seeing a shot rejected into the cheap seats.

A double pump dunk is a more difficult shot than a layup and an argument could be made that it is unwise to showboat when a safer shot is available. However, everyone knows how dispiriting a spectacular jam can be to the opposition. Same goes for a 30 foot three point shot – it's a bad shot if it misses but can be a game-changer if it goes.

To me, Wilt's emphatic blocks were among the most exciting and satisfying plays in basketball, and among the most memorable. He never forgot that basketball was entertainment as well as competition. His dramatic blocked shots helped keep the entire NBA in a perpetual state of intimidation. I think Wilt knew exactly what he was doing – and I'm glad he did it.

Wilt led the league in average minutes played per game nine times in his career and never averaged fewer than 42 minutes a game. Famously, he averaged 48.5 minutes per game in 1961-62, missing only 8 minutes all year because of an expulsion on technical fouls. (His average exceeded the 48 minutes of a complete game because of overtimes played.)

Inevitably, some criticized Wilt for this. His least favored coach, Butch van Breda Kolff, angered him by forcing him to sit against his wishes. Wilt insisted that he had difficulty warming up after in-game breaks, so he preferred to play the full 48 minutes, with little or no time spent on the bench.

Wilt's first coach in Philadelphia, Frank Maguire, remembered meeting with him before the 1961-62 season:

> *When Wilt came in, I asked him how long he'd like to play. He said, "Forever." I almost fell off my chair. I said, "No, Wilt, in a game." He said, "I don't ever have to come out of a game." And he didn't."*

Paradoxically, the retired Wilt wondered out loud why Maguire didn't rest him during that 48.5 minute per game season:

> *Just one game, 48 minutes a game is really enough, but playing a whole season 48 minutes a game? I mean when I look back in retrospect I say "What were they doing to me?" Jeez, there must have been some time I could have gotten a rest?*

Sometimes, Wilt liked to have it both ways.

In any case, Wilt's stamina and durability are among the most remarkable aspects of his legend. His career regular season and playoff averages are 45.8 mpg and 47.2 mpg, respectively. This regular season average is 7.5 more minutes than Michael Jordan's, 7.1 more than Lebron James's, and 3.5 more than Bill Russell's, who is number 2 all-time.

PLAYOFF NUMBERS

Wilt's haters often try to "prove" that he was a choker by pointing out that, though his rebounding numbers were higher in the playoffs and his assists about the same, his playoff scoring average is significantly lower than his regular season average - 30.1 vs. 22.5.

In addition, while Wilt's scoring numbers declined in the playoffs, they went up for players like Bill Russell and Michael Jordan. Surely this proves that Wilt choked in the playoffs?

Well, no. As I will try to show below, these numbers are very misleading for several reasons.

> *First, most of Wilt's playoff games occurred after his high scoring years had passed (he played 52 playoff games when he was the league's leading scorer and 108 games afterwards). This means that his low scoring years are disproportionately represented in his average.*

> *Second, most of his playoff appearances happened after the pace of the game had slowed (reducing points, rebounds, and assists for everyone).*

> *Third, tightened defense dramatically decreased team scoring in the playoffs, as will be shown below. This would have affected low post players more than perimeter players because defenses tended to sag toward the middle, especially in the days before 3-pointers (pre-1979).*

> *And fourth, Wilt's playing time only increased slightly in the playoffs, from 45.8 minutes per game in the regular season to 47.2 minutes in the playoffs – only a 1.4 minute increase. In contrast, most other star players increased their playing time by much more. For example: Bill Russell – 42.3 vs. 45.4 (a 3.1 minute increase); Michael Jordan - 38.3 vs. 41.8 (a 3.5 minute increase). More playing time meant more points, rebounds, and assists,*

Taking these factors one at a time, how can we be sure that we are comparing apples to apples?

We can rectify the imbalance between his high scoring and low scoring years by considering his average *average* points per game in the playoffs. This means counting all of his yearly averages as equal, regardless of how many games he played, rather than simply dividing his total playoff points by his total number of games.

This turns out to be a more respectable 24.8 ppg, rather than 22.5 ppg. His rebounding average *average* also becomes 24.8, by the way, rather than the listed average of 24.5.

Concerning the effect of the changing pace of the game: that works both ways. It inflates his early numbers while deflating his later ones. This sort of evens out, so let's leave that one alone.

The tighter defense and decrease in scoring during the playoffs affect everyone's stats in one way or another, but if we are comparing Wilt's regular season numbers with his playoff stats, then we need to make an adjustment.

The following table shows Chamberlain's teams' regular season and playoff scoring averages as well as his own. It also extrapolates his playoff averages to what they would likely have been if the playoff rate of scoring had been the same as during the regular season. This yields a career scoring average of 27.0 points per game – a drop of just over 3.1 points a game from his regular season average.

<u>Wilt's Team and Individual Scoring Averages for the Regular Season (rs) and Playoffs (po) Plus his Adjusted Playoff Points Per Game (adj. po)</u>

1959-60: 118.6 rs; 113.9 po – 37.6 rs/33.2 po - 34.6 adj. po

1960-61: 121.0 rs; 108.0 po – 38.4 rs/37.0 po - 41.5 adj. po

1961-62: 125.4 rs; 106.1 po – 50.4 rs/35.0 po - 41.4 adj. po

1963-64: 118.5 rs; 106.5 po – 36.9 rs/34.7 po - 38.6 adj. po

1964-65: 112.5 rs; 111.8 po – 34.7 rs/29.3 po - 29.5 adj. po

1965-66: 117.3 rs; 104.0 po – 33.5 rs/28.0 po - 31.6 adj. po

1966-67: 125.2 rs; 121.7 po – 24.1 rs/21.7 po - 22.3 adj. po

1967-68: 122.6 rs; 113.7 po – 24.3 rs/23.7 po - 25.6 adj. po

1968-69: 112.2 rs; 103.7 po – 20.5 rs/13.9 po - 15.0 adj. po

1969-70: 113.7 rs; 114.0 po – 27.3 rs/22.1 po - 22.0 adj. po

1970-71: 114.8 rs;   99.7 po – 20.7 rs/18.3 po - 21.1 adj. po

1971-72: 121.0 rs; 106.6 po – 14.8 rs/14.7 po - 16.7 adj. po

1972-73: 111.7 rs; 103.4 po – 13.2 rs/10.4 po - 11.2 adj. po

It may be argued that the modest decline in Wilt's adjusted scoring average should be expected considering the years Wilt was his team's principal scorer from the low post. Perimeter players tend to score more in the playoffs than post players because 1) they control the ball and 2) tighter, sagging defenses make it harder to get the ball inside.

This is borne out by the following numbers for perimeter, ball-handling players:

	Regular Season Average	Playoff Average
Jerry West	27.0	29.1
Michael Jordan	30.1	33.4
Sam Jones	17.7	18.9
Walt Frazier	18.9	20.7

In contrast, the following shows how inside players from Wilt's era tended to score less in the playoffs

	Regular Season Average	Playoff Average
Bob Lanier	20.1	18.6
Nate Thurmond	15.0	11.9
Walt Bellamy	20.1	18.5
Willis Reed	18.7	17.4

Bill Russell was an exception to this rule (16.2 points in the playoffs vs. 15.1 regular season), but his per 36 minute scoring averages for the regular season and playoffs were identical (12.8). Also, he tended to be an opportunistic scorer rather than a go-to option, with many of his points coming from offensive rebounds.

Because of the varying numbers of minutes played for different players, comparing their 36 minute averages seems to be the best way to go if we want to compare apples to apples. This actually hurts Wilt's numbers a bit because he played almost the entire game and presumably had to pace himself. In contrast, Kareem Abdul-Jabbar only averaged 36.8 minutes in the regular season for his career, and 37.3 in the playoffs.

In Wilt's case, I will use his scoring *average* average (24.8) for the playoffs rather than his actual average (22.5) in the table below. He was the only player discussed whose role changed dramatically during his prime and whose playoff scoring average was distorted by that fact.

It is also true that Kareem Abdul-Jabbar's numbers declined when he was in the twilight of his career, and that affects his numbers.

Michael Jordan never made the playoffs past age 34 and Bill Russell retired at that age.

<u>Career Average Statistics per 36 minutes for the</u>
<u>Regular Season/Playoffs</u>

	Points	Reb.	Ass.	FG%	FT%
Wilt Chamberlain	23.6/18.9*	18.0/18.6	3.5/3.2	54.0/52.2	51.1/46.5
Bill Russell	12.8/12.8	19.1/19.7	3.6/3.7	44.0/43.0	56.1/60.3
K. Abdul-Jabbar	24.1/23.4	10.9/10.1	3.5/3.1	55.9/53.3	72.1/74.0
Michael Jordan	28.3/28.8	5.9/5.5	4.9/4.9	49.7/48.7	83.5/82.8

*This number is based on Wilt's adjusted playoff scoring *average* average of 24.6. The actual (unadjusted) number, based on a preponderance of games late in his career, is 17.2.

In Wilt's case, the only significant drop is in points and, as I have argued, this is largely due to his position on the court and the nature of playoff defense. His rebounding actually increased during the playoffs and his other numbers only declined slightly.

Bill Russell's scoring per 36 minutes remained unchanged in the playoffs and his field goal percentage declined, but his other numbers were up slightly.

Kareem Abdul-Jabbar's numbers all declined during the playoffs, except for his free throw percentage. This is partly because, like Wilt, he played proportionally more playoff games late in his career than in his prime.

Michael Jordan's scoring increased by one half point per 36 minutes in the playoffs and his assists remained the same. All other numbers considered here declined slightly.

All in all, Wilt's playoff performance does not stand out in a negative way when compared to these other superstars.

As may be obvious, this is a complicated area of statistics and it would be dangerous to draw conclusions about who was clutch and who wasn't without looking at the numbers very carefully, and year by year.

In his first book, Wilt wrote the following:

It was one of the most curious sensations I'd ever experienced in my entire life. The Lakers had just beaten the Chicago Bulls, 95-92, to win the first round of the 1973 playoffs in Los Angeles. We had won in the final seconds of the final quarter of the final game, when I blocked a jump shot near the top of the key, grabbed the ball and fired a full-court pass to Gail Goodrich for a lay-up.

And yet, when it was all over, and I found myself, quite literally, with tears in my eyes, the tears were not tears of triumph and joy and exultation – or even relief – for myself and my teammates. The tears were tears of anguish – and they were for the Chicago Bulls...

Chicago, to be honest about it, had deserved to win...

(from Wilt: Just Like Any Other 7-Foot Black Millionaire Who Lives Next Door, *page 1)*

Chamberlain had a very strong sense of fair play, which was evident in many aspects of how he conducted himself on the court. He is said to have cheated at card games and checkers, but never at basketball. He has even been plausibly accused of limiting his own performance because his superior strength, size, and skill somehow gave him an "unfair" advantage.

Wilt was often blamed for not taking full advantage of Willis Reed's injury in game 7 of the 1970 championship series. When the injury occurred in game 5, Wilt even extended a helping hand to the fallen Reed. It was said that he was "too soft at heart, too fearful of his power to injure."

Bill Russell commented that "If I'm the one playing Willis when he comes out limping, it would only have emphasized my goal of beating them that much worse."

Chamberlain would not, as it was said about Russell, "do *anything it took* to win." To some this was a weakness in his game. To me, it was one of his more admirable qualities. The fact that he won so often simply by doing his best within the rules and without being utterly ruthless makes him a role model for those who see basketball as a game rather than a life or death struggle where the ends always justify the means.

Chamberlain was no *kamikaze,* though he would occasionally dive after loose balls. He wouldn't throw an elbow at an opponent's face or pull down his pants to get an edge – both of which happened to him more than once. Nor would he gloat over an opposing player after a dunk, or pound his chest or flex his biceps, nor curse a man's mother or sister or his manhood. He knew that basketball was a game. There have been some who have blamed Wilt for this – I admire him for it.

IMPACT ON GAME

Without question, the biggest impact that Wilt Chamberlain had on the NBA was keeping it afloat financially at a critical juncture. Many of the league's teams were on the verge of bankruptcy when he arrived.

To quote Oscar Robertson:

> *Wilt Chamberlain saved the league when he came into the league [in 1959]. If he didn't come along at exactly the time that he did and do all of the things that he accomplished then, I'm not sure the league would have survived and we'd even be talking about pro basketball now.*

Wilt's record-breaking heroics made him the first truly mainstream superstar in professional basketball, drawing many new fans and giving the league its first household name. However much Wilt hated the nickname, everyone knew who "Wilt the Stilt" was (he preferred to be called "Dipper").

He often appeared on television shows, such as *The Ed Sullivan Show* and *What's My Line?* and his exploits were covered by the major magazines and newspapers of the day. As mentioned above, he even wrote an article for *Look Magazine* explaining why he was leaving college a year early, and was paid $10,000 for it – more than the average NBA player's salary!

Chamberlain was able to demand and get unprecedented contracts, often much larger than what was publicly announced. He became the highest paid player in the league before he even played his first game, making 20% more than the reigning superstar, Bob Cousy. Wilt even claimed that he was promised 25% of the Philadelphia 76ers by its owner Ike Richman, though the agreement was verbal only and was not honored after Ike's death, to Wilt's long-lasting dismay.

From a basketball perspective, Wilt revolutionized the game, redefining the offensive role of the center position in much the same way that Russell redefined its defensive role. Not only did Wilt employ a wider range of moves than predecessors like George Mikan, Neil Johnston, and Bill Russell had utilized, he became his team's principal playmaker.

His dominance changed the game by inspiring a number of rule changes. In order to counter his abilities, the NBA widened the lane from 12 to 16 feet, outlawed offensive goaltending, and instituted the "3 seconds" rule, requiring an offensive player to leave the lane within 3 seconds if he has not taken a shot. Inbounding the ball over the top of the backboard was also made illegal as Wilt was capable of catching it above the rim and dropping it through the hoop. Leaping from the foul line to dunk free throws - something that probably only Wilt could do - was also outlawed.

And Wilt changed the culture as well. Before him, a seven footer was generally seen as a circus freak who was often assumed to be of below average intelligence. Few gawkers would want to be like him.

After Wilt Chamberlain, a seven footer, especially a young black one, is likely to be seen as a basketball player who might make a lot of money and enjoy an elite lifestyle – someone to be envied and admired.

As a role model for young players, Wilt profoundly influenced those who came after him, both in terms of playing style and personal demeanor. When Julius Erving is asked to name his top five all-time players, he stubbornly refuses to update the list he had in his youth: "Wilt Chamberlain, Oscar Robertson, Elgin Baylor [his favorite], Bill Russell, and Jerry West." These were the men he idolized and copied when he was learning the game, and he remains loyal to them to this day.

The generation after "The Doctor," including Michael Jordan, emulated him – without necessarily knowing that they were also imitating Wilt. And they in turn were emulated by the likes of Kobe Bryant and Lebron James. The chain goes unbroken; each generation adding new skills - and abandoning some old ones - but no generation truly surpasses the ones before it; it simply reinvents them.

There is an analogy in warfare. The modern day soldier has weapons that far surpass those of the Roman legionnaire, the Medieval knight, or the Native American warrior. But he or she does not excel those predecessors in courage, resourcefulness, or determination. Some tools of the trade get left behind, like swords, crossbows, wooden spears – and two handed set shots - but the physical, mental, and emotional challenges and the opportunities for greatness remain the same.

3. TEAM SUCCESS

How is team success measured? Some might say championship rings, but that is misleading, as I will argue below. I propose that overall playoff success is the best measure. Winning a ring takes a team made up of talented players that complement each other and play well together, great coaching, and a lot of luck. Most championship series are highly competitive and often come right down to the wire. Losing a ring in the final seconds of the seventh game by a few points after a contested call doesn't mean that the losing team or its star player is a loser.

In my opinion, championships are overrated. It takes a lot of hard work, luck, and (especially) money to put together a championship team, and there is only so much that individual players can do about this. A great many superb players have played with grace and dignity throughout their careers and never come close. The NBA draft system was even set up to ensure that the best players go to the worst teams, so mediocre players have actually had a better chance of becoming champs than their more talented peers.

Wilt is often labelled a "loser" because he "only" won two NBA championships in his 14 year career. In my opinion, far more was expected of him than should ever be expected of one man in a team sport. Consider whether any of the following athletes who won fewer professional championships than Wilt are or should be called losers:

John Stockton (0), Oscar Robertson (1), Karl Malone (0), Charles Barkley (0), Hank Aaron (1), Willie Mays (1), Ted Williams (0), Elgin Baylor (0), George Gervin (0), Patrick Ewing (0), Dirk Nowitzki (1), Ernie Banks (0), Barry Bonds (0), Ty Cobb (0), Ken Griffey Jr. (0), Allen Iverson (0), Harmon Killebrew (0), Dan Marino (0), Willie McCovey (0), Reggie Miller (0), Steve Nash (0), O. J. Simpson (0), Dominique Wilkins (0), Fran Tarkenton (0).

If we set aside rings (of which Wilt had as many or more than any non-Celtic during his career) and look at playoff success, it turns out that Wilt had far more than most superstars - more than Jordan, Kareem, Bird, Kobe, Shaq, Lebron – more than anyone, in fact, except Russell and Magic.

I came up with a way of measuring this. I looked at the following superstar players' careers and awarded three points for a ring, 2 points for losing in the finals, and one point for losing in the semifinals to the eventual champion. Then I divided the total of these points by the number of years in a player's career to see what their average playoff success was <u>per year</u>.

The results are given below. Note that Wilt Chamberlain (supposedly lacking in playoff success) was more successful in the playoffs than anyone but Russell (who played on the most polished team ever) and Magic (who played with Kareem for a decade and never won a championship without him):

<u>Playoff Success through 2017-18 Season</u>

Bill Russell: 2.78
Magic Johnson: 1.77
Wilt Chamberlain: 1.54
Lebron James: 1.47
Kareem Abdul-Jabbar: 1.45
Jerry West: 1.43
Michael Jordan: 1.33
Larry Bird: 1.08
Kobe Bryant: 1.00
Shaquille O'Neal: 0.89

Suddenly Chamberlain doesn't look like such a "loser."

Now, it is true that there were fewer teams in Wilt's day so there was a higher probability of making it to the finals or conference finals. However, Wilt spent seven years in the same conference as the Boston Celtics and, though his team was generally believed to be the second best in the league, it was barred from the finals - except in 1967 when it eliminated Boston and won the championship.

Also, success is success. Few people blame Bill Russell for playing when there were only 8 teams in the league, or Michael Jordan for winning rings when the league was full of weak expansion teams.

Wilt's teams only failed to make the playoffs once in his career, in 1962-63 when his Warriors team went 31-49 in their first year in San Francisco after losing their 2nd and 3rd best scorers (Tom Gola and Paul Arizin) and their coach (Frank Maguire).

4. WHY PEOPLE HATED GOLIATH

Wilt's parents raised him to be a nice guy and, for the most part, he was. NBA player and coach Jack McMahon once commented:

... The best thing that happened to the NBA is that God made Wilt a nice person... he could have killed us all with his left hand.

Many people who knew Wilt have commented on his friendly, generous personality and there are countless stories that reveal Wilt's decency and kindness towards others. Here are just two:

Paul Arizin was a teammate of Wilt's in his first few years in Philadelphia. In 1993, Paul's granddaughter Stephanie wrote a fan letter to Chamberlain asking for his autograph, but the letter was mislaid and not opened for three years. When Wilt finally read the letter, he phoned Stephanie, then 14 years old, and they hit it off.

When Wilt told Stephanie's father how much he had enjoyed the conversation, he was informed that the young girl had terminal cancer, which she had not even mentioned in their conversation. For the last 15 months of Stephanie's life, Wilt called her on the phone almost every single Friday.

Much less dramatically, but to indicate the many small things that Wilt did for people, there is a story about his interaction with his coach Frank Maguire, recounted by Frank in *Tall Tales*, by Terry Pluto:

One night we were on the road. We had lost. It was about two in the morning. I had gotten a terrible hotel room, and I was standing in the hall. Wilt saw me and asked what was wrong. I said, "Look at this room, it's like a shoebox." Wilt grabbed my key, then gave me his key. "I've got a room twice that size at the end of the hall, Coach. It's all yours." Then he shut the door to my old room in my face, the point being that he didn't want any arguments. He wanted me to take his room.

There are many other stories that illustrate Wilt's "behind the scenes" acts of kindness. He was a huge supporter of women's sports, including basketball, volleyball, softball, and track and field, though he did not make a public show of it. When Wilt died, the outstanding athlete Jackie Joyner-Kersee asked to attend his funeral, saying that her career would not have been possible without his help.

Among his many charities – supported without hoopla or media coverage - Wilt was a founding member of Operation Smile, the charity that repairs cleft palates in children around the world. He also supported rehabilitation programs for inmates at Sing Sing prison.

When Wilt made a television commercial with Bill Russell, Kareem Abdul-Jabbar, Bill Walton, and Shaquille O'Neal in 1992, celebrating the latter's entry into the NBA, Walton gave Wilt credit for making the meeting a pleasant one. As he put it:

> *I think it was Wilt Chamberlain's magnanimous personality and his humility. Wilt has such an outgoing and effervescent personality. He's just a... he's a special person. The other guys are special basketball players.*

Of course, there are stories that put Wilt in a less favorable light, but most of them concern words rather than deeds. Jerry West said of Wilt that he was a "complex... very nice person."

So why does Wilt have such a bad reputation?

In the 1950s and early 1960s, professional athletes – especially black professional athletes – were expected to be humble, self-effacing, and grateful for their success. And most of them were. The most visible exceptions were Cassius Clay (later known as Muhammad Ali) and Wilt Chamberlain.

Actually, Wilt was modest and soft-spoken most of the time. But when he was seriously mistreated, he stood up for himself, and sometimes he went too far for public taste. For example, he wrote a pair of articles for *Sport Illustrated* in 1965 entitled "My

Life in the Bush Leagues" in which he vented his frustrations over many things, including his treatment by the league, his coaches, fellow players, fans, and the world in general. Many people were offended by the articles and he was fined by the NBA for his outburst, which was perceived as "detrimental to the best interest of the league."

He reportedly could be a "pain in the ass" and a shameless braggart, prone to exaggeration and very reluctant to admit when he was wrong about something, no matter how trivial. Too often, his efforts to explain and defend himself made him appear petty, conceited, and ungrateful.

Some sportswriters like to spin their narratives into morality plays, where good triumphs and evil is vanquished. In support of their fiction, they tend to simplify complex situations and turn individuals into archetypes. All too often, Wilt was turned into a villain and his losses into retribution for his affronts and weaknesses.

Wilt famously claimed that this was partly because "Nobody Loves Goliath."

I would say "nobody" is too strong a word, but there was a lot of truth in that. He was just too big, too strong, too talented, too overwhelming. We were all children once, frightened of a world full of people who were bigger and stronger than ourselves and resentful of anyone who was too powerful and seemed to revel in their superiority. It is natural to root for David, for the underdog, because we were all underdogs once and there is a relief in seeing the mighty brought low.

Wilt was so much stronger, faster, and a better leaper than almost anyone else in the league, that it seemed that he had an unfair advantage. Too many expected him to win championships all by himself.

It must be said: One reason that Wilt was excoriated by the press and others during his playing days and after had to do with race. White sportswriters and fans in the 1950s and

60s were not ready for a wealthy black superstar who lived ostentatiously, thoroughly dominated the league statistically, and dated white women – lots of white women – at a time when interracial marriage was illegal in many parts of the U. S. (these laws were finally declared unconstitutional in 1967). He was a sort of latter day Jack Johnson, but more fortunate in that the laws were increasingly on his side.

As a black man who grew up when Jim Crow was still very active in much of the country, Wilt was called upon to justify himself in response to a segment of the population who considered him to be inferior because of his race. This was a major motivating factor for Bill Russell, whose intensity on the basketball court was very much an "in your face" response to white oppression.

Wilt had also grown up as a sort of walking sideshow, laughed at because of his extreme height and early awkwardness. According to biographer Robert Cherry's informants, Wilt was unable to find a date in high school and was considered by some to be an "ugly child." So it should be no surprise that when he grew into his full attractiveness, he was anxious to let everyone know about his success both on and off the court.

When criticized, Wilt tended to respond, not with anger or counterattacks, but with boasts and exaggerations. His infamous claim to have slept with 20,000 women falls in this category.

Wilt is remembered as a braggart. This was partly to counter unfair criticism, but also, perhaps, because of a sometimes awkward attempt to emulate the braggadocio of the transcendent black athlete of his generation – Muhammad Ali.

Elgin Baylor made an interesting point about the black men of his and Wilt's generation. He remarked that he and Wilt argued about everything when they were teammates, but added: "We were good friends and we respected one another. But there's a thing about black culture some people don't understand – it's always one-upmanship. You never let the guy get one up on you."

But Wilt Chamberlain has been denigrated by more than his own contemporaries, In more recent times, I've heard sports pundits who weren't even born when he stopped playing pontificate about his shortcomings and dismiss him as an over-rated player whose records were the result of playing a primitive game in a weak league.

Skip Bayliss, who is four months older than this writer and should know better, recently repeated the old saw that Bill Russell "owned" Wilt and then asked rhetorically if Wilt "ever played any defense."

Chamberlain was probably the greatest shot-blocker and defensive rebounder in the history of the game. Even Bill Russell – by most accounts the greatest defensive center in history – said that, late in his career, Wilt was playing that role better than he ever did. Bayliss's question was like asking if Michael Jordan ever bothered to score.

Boston Celtics fanboy Bill Simmons, who was all of 3 years old when Wilt retired, dedicated a section of his book about basketball to "proving" that Bill Russell was better than Wilt Chamberlain. How anyone can make such a claim without having seen more than a few hours of video of either player's career escapes me.

Simmons tried to refute the argument that Russell only won more championships than Wilt because he had better teammates. That is missing the point entirely. Russell almost always had a better TEAM, partly because of his own efforts but also because of better coaching, an established winning tradition, and the fact that his team stayed together longer.

Red Auerbach, the brilliant coach of the Boston Celtics for 9 of their championships, waged effective psychological warfare against Wilt. He labelled him "a giant," his tone of voice implying that Wilt was a little more or a little less than human and more than a little threatening.

This touched a nerve. Because Wilt was made into an object of fear, many delighted in his losses and in any perceived weaknesses in his game, dwelling on them and exaggerating them.

Unfortunately, a lot of this got into Wilt's head and made him defensive. He was not shy about recalling his many records and individual accomplishments. Wilt's accomplishments were well-known. By bragging about them, and even exaggerating them, Wilt made himself into a target of ridicule and derision, and ultimately detracted from the impressive truth of his greatness.

When his Kansas team lost the NCAA finals in three overtimes to North Carolina, Wilt felt personally responsible, something that he never fully got over. He was even nervous about being booed when he attended a Kansas ceremony to retire his number in 1999 – 42 years after the defeat.

To some extent, Wilt himself believed that he should have been able to carry his team to victory and that every loss was a personal failure on his part. When his teams lost, and then lost again, all he could do was try to justify himself by pointing to his statistics, to prove that he had done his best.

The more times he was unfavorably compared to Bill Russell and blamed for his team's failure to overcome the Celtics, the more urgently he stressed his statistical dominance. How else could he justify his salary and celebrity?

Wilt was disliked for being independent, outspoken, and self-determining. He came across as a proud and outspoken athlete who stood up for himself and wasn't afraid to blow his own horn. He was also a man who shared his innermost feelings and sensitivities publicly. In other words, Wilt was way, way ahead of his time.

FALLACY #1 – BILL RUSSELL OWNED WILT

If, like Kareem Abdul-Jabbar, Wilt had spent the bulk of his career without a serious rival at the center position, his stature as the greatest of his time would be much more obvious than it is. Instead, he shared the court for 10 years with Bill Russell, arguably the greatest defensive player ever, who was a top three all-time rebounder, excellent passer, and superb team player. His team also just happened to be perfectly suited for his skills, brilliantly coached, and wonderfully well-balanced.

This shouldn't have taken anything away from Wilt, but as Russell and the Celtics won most of the championships, it gave those who worship rings and think that winning is everything an excuse to berate Wilt and call him a loser who was "owned" by his great rival.

This is a lie that was promulgated by sportswriters of the 50s and 60s who saw the rivalry between Wilt's teams and the Boston Celtics as some kind of Shakespearean drama. Wilt was cast as the self-centered behemoth and Bill as the unselfish team player – David to Wilt's Goliath. This was – and is – nonsense.

I certainly don't intend to argue against the greatness of Bill Russell. Thanks to the Celtics success (11 championships during his 13 years), there is considerable video footage to reveal what a devastating shot-blocker, magnificent rebounder, and offensive facilitator he was.

Wilt himself picked Russell as the best center ever because of his superb skills and the way they fit into the team concept. He argued that his own overwhelming abilities sometimes detracted from the effectiveness of his teammates. As Russell put it when asked who he would pick first from the trio of himself, Wilt, or Michael Jordan, "You pick Bill Russell because he will never distort your defense or your offense."

Bill and Wilt played against each other 143 times. Wilt won the personal battle statistically by a wide margin, averaging an astonishing 28.7 rebounds and 28.7 points against Bill, who averaged 23.7 rebounds and 14.5 points against Wilt.

Chamberlain even set the all-time NBA rebounding record of 55 boards on November 24, 1960 against Russell and the Celtics.

During the years that Wilt played against Russell, he averaged 33.5 points and 24.5 rebounds against the league as a whole, showing that Russ and the Boston defense did affect his scoring adversely, though not his rebounding. And Russell's Celtics won the team war, with 86 victories against 57 defeats (66.2% - to be compared with their overall 1958-1969 winning percentage of 70.7%).

This did not make Bill Russell a better player than Wilt Chamberlain; it made the Celtics the better team. And what a team! They were hard to beat in Russell's day. The core players on the Celtics played together – and won together – for many years.

In the 1968 playoffs, at the end of Wilt's tenure in Philadelphia, Russell led a team that had a combined total of 52 years' experience playing with him, including 12 years with the same coach. By comparison, Wilt's teammates had a combined total of 33 years playing with him, including 4 years with his coach, Alex Hannum. The following year, when Wilt was with the Lakers, the totals were 64 years (Russell) and 10 years (Wilt).

Much has been written about the relative quality of Bill's Celtic teammates vs. that of Wilt's teammates, comparing the number and caliber of Hall of Famers who played with each. For the most part, this is irrelevant; a team is far more than the sum of its parts. Certainly, the Celtics had many great players (e.g. Bob Cousy, John Havlicek, Sam Jones, K. C. Jones, Bill Sharman, Tom "Satch" Sanders, Tom Heinsohn, and many others), but it was their coaching and teamwork that set them apart.

I grew up in the Virginia suburbs of Washington, D.C. and my favorite team in the late 1960s and 1970s – after whatever team Wilt played for, that is – was the Baltimore/Washington Bullets. In 1974, the Bullets tied for the best record in the league (60-22) and made it to the finals against the underdog Golden State Warriors (48-34).

The Bullets were favored to win the series by a huge margin, based on their record and their roster, which included superstars Elvin Hayes and Wes Unseld, plus Phil Chenier, Kevin Porter, and a good mix of veterans and talented young players.

The Warriors had a mediocre regular season record, only one superstar (Rick Barry), plus an old Bill Bridges, a very young Jamaal Wilkes, and a comparatively unheralded center named Clifford Ray. On paper, the Bullets had a much better team with superior talent.

Well, the predictions were correct; the match was an uneven one. But it was the Warriors who swept my Bullets in four straight games. Personnel aside, they were the better TEAM. They played together and, like the Celtics, they were much better than they looked on paper.

HEAD TO HEAD FINAL PLAYOFF GAMES

The Boston Celtics and Wilt's teams met in the playoffs a total of 8 times. The Celtics won 7 of these. However, they won the deciding games of those 7 series by a total of only 23 points – just over 3 points per game.

In the total of 8 playoff series-ending games, Wilt's teams actually <u>outscored</u> the Celtics overall by one point, thanks to a blowout win in 1967.

Wilt and Russell faced each other in do-or-die playoff games fifteen times during their careers. Wilt's teams won 4, Russell's won 11. Their comparative numbers for these must-win games are shown below.

<u>Do or Die games between Wilt and Russell</u>
<u>(W=Wilt, R=Russell)</u>

1960 Game 5 – 128-107 Philly
        W- 50 pts. (22/42 fg, 6/14 ft)   35 reb. 2 ass.
        R- 22 pts   (9/16 fg, 4/6 ft)   27 reb. 4 ass.

1960 Game 6 – 119-117 Boston
     W- 26 pts. (8/18 fg, 10/16 ft) 24 reb. 0 ass.
     R- 25 pts. (11/26 fg, 3/4 ft) 25 reb. 3 ass.

1962 Game 6 - 109-99 Philly
     W- 32 pts. (12/29 fg, 8/10 ft) 21 reb. 1 ass.
     R- 19 pts. (8/21 fg, –3/6 ft) 22 reb, 2 ass.

1962 Game 7 - 109-107 Boston
     W- 22 pts. (7/15 fg, 8/9 ft)   22 reb, 3 ass.
     R- 19 pts. (7/14 fg, 5/5 ft)   22 reb. 1 ass.

1964 Game 5 – 109-105 Boston
     W- 30 pts. (12/28 fg, 6/13 ft) 27 reb. 2 ass.
     R- 14 pts. (5/11 fg, 4/5 ft) 26 reb. 6 ass.

1965 Game 6 - 112-106 Philly
     W- 30 pts. (13/22 fg, 4/8 ft) 26 reb. 4 ass.
     R- 22 pts. (8/19 fg, 6/10 ft) 21 reb. 5 ass.

1965 Game 7 – 110-109 Boston
     W- 30 pts. (12/15 fg, 6/13 ft) 32 reb. 2 ass.
     R- 15 pts,   (7/16 fg, 1/2 ft) 29 reb. 8 ass.

1966 Game 5 – 120-112 Boston
     W- 46 pts. (19/34 fg, 8/25 ft) 34 reb. 1 ass.
     R- 18 pts. (6/11 fg, 6/10 ft) 31 reb. 6 ass.

1967 Game 4 – 121-117 Boston
     W- 20 pts. (8/18 fg, 4/10 ft) 22 reb. 10 ass.
     R- 9 pts. (2/7 fg, 5/9 ft)   28 reb. 5 ass.

1967 Game 5 – 140-116 Philly
     W- 29 pts. (10/16 fg, 9/17 ft) 36 reb. 13 ass.
     R- 4 pts. (2/5 fg, 0/1 ft)   21 reb. 7 ass.

1968 Game 5 – 122-104 Boston
     W- 28 pts. (4/9 fg, 6/15 ft)   30 reb. 7 ass.
     R- 8 pts. (4/10 fg, 0/0 ft)   24 reb. 4 ass.

1968 Game 6 – 114-106 Boston
     W- 20 pts. (6/21 fg, 8/22 ft) 27 reb. 8 ass.
     R- 17 pts. (6/13 fg, 5/7 ft) 31 reb. 5 ass.

1968 Game 7 – 100-96 Boston
    W- 14 pts. (4/9 – 6/15)   34 reb. 5 ass.
    R- 12 pts. (4/6 – 4/10)   26 reb. 5 ass.

1969 Game 6 – 99-90 Boston
    W- 8 pts. (1/5 fg, 6/10 ft)   18 reb. 4 ass.
    R- 9 pts. (3/8 fg, 3/3 ft)   19 reb. 2 ass.

1969 Game 7 – 108-106 Boston
    W- 18 pts. (7/8 fg, 4/13 ft)   27 reb. 3 ass.
    R- 6 pts. (2/7 fg, 2/4 ft)   21 reb. 6 ass.

Though the Boston dynasty won 11 of these 15 must-win games, the comparative per game statistics for Wilt versus Russell are not one-sided in the same direction:

	FT	FTA	FT%	FG	FGA	FG%	PPG	RPG	APG
Wilt	6.6	14.0	47.1%	9.7	19.3	50.2%	26.9	27.7	4.3
Russell	3.5	5.5	63.4%	5.6	12.7	44.2%	14.6	24.9	4.6

It is clear that Bill Russell held his own pretty well against Chamberlain – and that Chamberlain held his own pretty well against Russell, the best defensive center of all time, and the Celtics, the best defensive team in the league.

These two men were titans of the game, and their matchups were thrilling to watch. Both almost always played superbly – and, clearly, neither one "owned" the other. A player does not "own" another player by whom one is out-scored, out-rebounded, and out-shot in must-win games.

Russell was generally given the nod in these contests for the simple reason that, rightly or wrongly, so much more was expected of Wilt. Given the fact that Bill Russell was named MVP of the league 5 times to Wilt's 4, one might wonder why, especially when many of the same people who voted Russell the best were the hardest on Wilt's performances.

As an aside, it should be said that individual statistics for NBA games in this era (at least) are not always reliable. Harvey Pollack told a tale about an experience in Boston:

I went to a Boston-Warriors game in the Boston Garden and secretly kept track of the rebounds of both Wilt and Russell. When the game ended, I went to the press table and asked what the rebound totals were for Wilt and Russell. The response: "Russell 35, Wilt 22." My response, "Well my totals are Wilt 34, Russell 21." They sat open mouthed when I produced my evidence of the time and type of every rebound that each player had.

(from The Greatest, *by Harvey Pollack, NBA Encyclopedia, Playoff Edition, 2006)*

FALLACY #2 – WILT WAS SELFISH AND ONLY CARED ABOUT HIS STATS

Any player who says he doesn't care about his statistics is not being truthful. Statistics have a lot to do with contract size, awards and accolades, and fan appeal. Of course, a player who scores a lot of points may arouse the envy of his teammates and risks being accused of selfishness.

The key question, however, is whether the player is scoring for the best interests of his team and in accordance with his coach's instructions. The answer in the case of Wilt Chamberlain was almost always "yes."

For the first 7 years of his career, Wilt was the greatest scorer in NBA history, by far. His coach Frank Maguire asked him to average 50 points in 1961-62 – and his teammates to support that goal. He did and they did and the team enjoyed great success.

But then, in the 1966-67 season, Wilt's new coach Alex Hannum asked him to change his game radically; to sacrifice his scoring and become a playmaker. Wilt complied, averaging 7.8 assists per game and letting his scoring average drop from 33.5 to 24.1 – and the team knocked off Boston and won the NBA championship.

Perhaps this ultimate sacrifice is all that is needed to prove that Wilt Chamberlain was a team player. I can think of no other superstar in the history of the NBA who willingly changed his game so completely to suit the needs of his team.

So why is Wilt still remembered by some as a selfish stat hog? Two reasons:

First, Red Auerbach tried to get into Wilt's head – and give his team an edge – by claiming vociferously that all Wilt cared about was his numbers. He created the fiction that Bill Russell was a team player who only cared about winning while Chamberlain was a loser because he put his statistics first.

Auerbach must have known this wasn't true. He witnessed the change in Wilt's style of play under Hannum and he knew Wilt well enough before his NBA career that he had tried to move heaven and earth to make him a Celtic. He also knew that Bill Russell cared just as much about statistics as Wilt did – only he had the luxury of dwelling on his numbers of wins and championships rather than points and rebounds. Russell could never have matched Wilt's individual numbers, so he focused on the kind of numbers that Wilt couldn't match.

Auerbach's psychological warfare might have come to nothing if not for reason number two. Wilt *was* obsessed with his numbers – but not because they were more important to him than winning; because they were the only way he could justify his being the best paid and most famous player in the world and prove that he had done everything he had been asked to do in order to defeat the Celtics.

As a proud and sensitive man, Wilt emphasized his productivity because he couldn't point to championships like Russell could. The more Wilt was criticized and called a loser, the more he tried to prove his worth by citing his numbers; and the more he seemed to support Auerbach's claims against him. But seriously, what else could he point to, without denigrating his coaches or teammates, in order to excuse himself for not winning a ring every year as many people thought he should?

FALLACY #3 – WILT PLAYED AGAINST WHITE MIDGETS

In 1960, the average American male stood just over 5 feet 8 inches tall. In 2018, the average was 5 foot 9 inches – less than one inch taller.

But what about professional basketball players in the NBA?

In Wilt's day, players were measured barefoot. This changed in or about the year he retired and players have been measured with shoes on ever since. It is estimated that shoes add from 1 to 1-1/2 inches to a player's height.

In 1961-1962, when Wilt averaged 50.4 points and 25.7 rebounds per game, there was a total of 18 centers on the rosters of the 9 NBA teams. Their average height <u>without</u> shoes was 6 feet 9.94 inches.

In 2017-2018, there was a total of 114 centers on the rosters of 30 NBA teams. Their average height <u>with shoes</u> was 6 feet 10.88 inches.

The average height of all players in the NBA has gone from a shade under 6 feet 5 1/2 inches <u>without</u> shoes in 1962 to a shade under 6 feet 7 inches <u>with shoes</u> in 2018.

This means that the average center in 2017-2018 was slightly *shorter* than the average center in 1961-1962, and the average player was about the same height in both eras, or perhaps as much as ½ inch taller in 2018.

It's been argued that Bill Russell would have been too small to play center in today's NBA and would have to play forward. Not true! Bill Russell was 6' 9 1/2" and, by modern measuring standards (in shoes), would be listed at 6'11" today. With his rare psychological gifts, a body like Kevin Garnett's, his speed, reflexes, and jumping ability, and his rebounding, passing, and shot-blocking skills, he would be one of the best centers in the NBA today, if not *the* best.

There's a wonderful video of a feeble, 83 year old Bill Russell appearing with a cane in 2017 to receive the NBA Life Achievement Award. He pauses to appraise a line-up on stage of Hall-of-Fame centers – David Robinson, Dikembe Mutombo, Shaquille O'Neal, Kareem Abdul-Jabbar, and Alonzo Mourning. Then he points at each one and says to them all: "I would kick your ass." And the man who held his own against Wilt Chamberlain probably would have done just that.

Enough said about height.

Weight is a different matter. Wilt's playing weight in his peak years was between 290 and 310 pounds. At the time, he was one of the very few players to lift weights. It was generally believed at that time that lifting weights would spoil a shooter's "touch." Chamberlain was one of the pioneers who changed this way of thinking, though it is possible that it affected his free throw shooting (see above).

However, Wilt's game depended far more on finesse and leaping ability than on brute strength, and his weight didn't give him the advantage it might have had he played more like Shaquille O'Neal. On the other hand, if he had played like Shaq, he would have fouled out on a regular basis as offensive charging fouls were far more stringently called in his era than in Shaq's.

The average weight of an NBA player in 1962 was about 204 pounds as opposed to about 217 pounds in 2018. However, many lighter players have continued to excel during the interim (consider George Gervin, Steve Nash, Michael Jordan, Kobe Bryant, John Stockton, Steph Curry, Kevin Durant) and the jury is out on whether greater weight is truly an advantage, especially in an open, run and gun style of play, such as that of 1962 – and of 2019!

The racial makeup of the NBA is another matter. Today, the league is almost 75% black. For much of Wilt's day, there was an unofficial limit of 4 black players per 11 man team (36%). However, this limit had been abandoned by the mid to late 1960s. The 1966-67 Boston Celtics team that Wilt's team defeated on its way to the championship was 50% black and the New York Knicks team that Wilt's Lakers defeated for the championship in 1972 was 67% black. Overall, the NBA was 65% black when Wilt retired.

FALLACY #4 – WILT WAS UNCOACHABLE

Bill Russell played for two coaches during his 13-year NBA career: Red Auerbach (10 years), with whom he had a close relationship and by whom he was always treated deferentially, and himself (3 years).

Wilt, on the other hand, played for a motley crew of eight different coaches, some of whom he liked and respected, others not so much. Each had his own ideas about what Wilt's role on the team should be and, although Wilt had his share of disagreements with coaches and sometimes went more public about them than he should have, he did something that perhaps no other superstar has ever done: he dramatically changed his game to suit his coach's wishes.

When asked to carry the scoring load early in his career, he set records that no one else has ever approached. Frank Maguire challenged him to average 50 points a game at the beginning of the 1961-62 season, and Wilt reached that goal.

When Alex Hannum asked him to sacrifice much of his scoring and concentrate on becoming a playmaker, he responded by becoming the only center in NBA history to lead the league in total assists.

And when Bill Sharman asked Wilt to "play like Bill Russell," curtailing his scoring even further and concentrating on defense, rebounding, and starting a guard–oriented, fast-breaking offense, Wilt set a still-unbroken record for field goal percentage (72.7%), led his team to a new record for regular season wins (69) and an NBA title (in 1971-72), and led the league in rebounds at the age of 36.

Listed below are the coaches Wilt played for, with their

lifetime coaching records in the NBA and his assessment of them
as coaches and men (paraphrased).

*Neil Johnston (1959-1961) - 154 pro games (95-59) –
"bad guy, bad coach"*

*Frank McGuire (1961-1962) - 80 pro games (49-31) –
"great guy, great coach"*

*Bob Feerick (1962-1963) - 148 pro games (68-85) –
"great guy, bad coach"*

*Alex Hannum (1963-1965, 1966-1968) - 1213 pro games
(649-564) – "good guy, great coach"*

*Dolph Schayes (1965-1966) - 323 pro games (151-172) –
"good guy, bad coach"*

*Butch van Breda Kolff (1968-1969) - 603 pro games (287-
316) – "bad guy, bad coach"*

*Joe Mullaney (1969-1971) - 566 pro games (322-244) –
"good guy, good coach"*

*Bill Sharman (1971-1974) - 819 pro games (466-353) –
"good guy, great coach"*

FALLACY #5 – WILT WAS A BAD TEAMMATE

Sports pundit Bill Simmons tried to denigrate Wilt by
pointing out that, when asked if they wanted Wilt to join their
team, the Lakers voted no. However, this probably had more
to do with a reluctance to share the spotlight and scoring
opportunities than with an aversion to Wilt as a person. Wilt
was always surrounded by intense press coverage and general
hoopla, which players could reasonably resent and/or see as a
distraction.

There was also the oft-repeated truism that Wilt got more than his share of the credit when his team won, as well as more than his share of the blame when it lost. As his teams tended to win more than lose, this was not a good bargain for his teammates.

Let's put it this way, having Wilt Chamberlain join your team usually meant that your points, rebounds, assists, and/or minutes would decrease.

As Wilt himself was keenly aware, contracts were based on performance, which were ultimately based on statistics. So few players trying to feed their families would invite the chance to see their numbers go down, even if it meant more team success.

This was an issue for Guy Rodgers when his coach (Frank Maguire) told him that his job was to get the ball to Mr. Chamberlain. Guy asked if the coach would vouch for him at contract time if his reduced point production became an issue. Maguire promised that he would.

Wilt's teammates famously underperformed in the playoffs. Consider their combined shooting percentages statistics for the first 6 post-seasons of Wilt's career: .382, .380, .354, .352, .352, and .332. By comparison, Wilt's percentages were .496, .469, .467, .543, .530, and .509.

Why did this happen? Because the opposing teams tightened their defense on Wilt, double and triple teaming him, and forcing his teammates to assume a much greater portion of the scoring burden than they were used to in the regular season. This threw his teams out of their offense and Wilt's teammates in the early years just weren't able to adjust.

Many of Wilt's teammates and some of his coaches became life-long friends. One of his best personal friends was Bob Billings, a teammate at Kansas, with whom Wilt stayed in touch for the rest of his life. 25 years after his retirement, Wilt continued to socialize with his former coach Alex Hannum.

Good friends from his professional playing days included former teammates Al Attles, Billy Cunningham, Paul Arizin, Tom Gola, Meadowlark Lemon, Jerry West, Elgin Baylor, Bill Bridges, Nate Thurmond, and Keith Erickson (who introduced him to volleyball). He was also on very good terms with Earl "The Pearl" Monroe, Bob Lanier, Bill Walton, and Bill Russell - until Russell attacked him after the 1969 finals, a rift that was patched up in the 1990s. When Wilt passed away, almost all of these former players attended his funeral and/or memorial services.

There are three kinds of people: those who like to lead; those who like to follow; and those who prefer to follow their own path, with or without company. Wilt was the last of these. He led by example, but he didn't need followers and he would not be a follower. He often led by doing, but he was not the sort of person to call team meetings or direct his teammates on the court, though there were exceptions to both of these rules. In the eyes of some, this made him an imperfect team player.

When Wilt had the right teammates and they were playing together as an integrated unit, his teams won NBA titles and compiled the best won-loss records up to that time – the champion 1967 Philadelphia 76ers (68-13) and the 1972 Los Angeles Lakers (69-13). This proves that Wilt could play and be successful in a team structure, when the coaching and personnel allowed it.

FALLACY #6 – WILT WASN'T CLUTCH

Perhaps one of the most interesting clutch performances of all time didn't involve the final score. With 46 seconds left in a game that Wilt's team led by 21 points, the entire crowd was on its feet, screaming for him to score. His opponents were doing everything they possibly could to stop him and Wilt was exhausted, but he made it. He scored on a dunk – for 100 points!

What if he hadn't been able to score and wound up with "only" 98?

The truth is, centers are usually at a disadvantage when it

comes to being heroes in the clutch. Before the 3 point shot especially, defenses tended to sag toward the middle at crunch time and the ball tended to stay in the hands of guards. Bigs were needed to protect the rim on defense and grab offensive rebounds on offense.

Nevertheless, Wilt had his moments. Here are just a few of his memorable "clutch" performances:

> *- With five minutes left in game seven of the 1964 Western Division finals against the St. Louis Hawks, Wilt ensured a Warriors' victory by blocking three consecutive shots - by Hall-of-Famers Richie Guerin, Bob Pettit, and Cliff Hagan. Chamberlain's teammate Nate Thurmond - one of the greatest defensive centers of all time - said that Wilt's performance "not only won us the division title but also gave me a model to follow the rest of my career as far as playing defensive center is concerned."*

> *- In Game 7 of the 1965 Eastern Conference finals against the reigning champion Boston Celtics, Wilt (30 points, 32 rebounds) took over at the end of the 4th quarter, scoring 8 of his team's last 10 points, including 2 clutch free throws, and bringing the 76ers within one point (110-109) with the ball under their basket and 5 seconds left. Wilt's teammate Hal Greer inbounded the ball – and John Havlicek stole it.*

> *- In Game 6 of the 1972 Western Conference Finals against Kareem Abdul-Jabbar's defending champion Milwaukee Bucks, Wilt went for 20 points and 24 rebounds and led the Lakers to a come-from-behind victory, overcoming a 10 point 4th quarter deficit. He was praised for beating Kareem down court on fast breaks and Jerry West called it "the greatest ball-busting performance I've ever seen."*

> *- Wilt won his second championship in Game 5 of the 1972 finals against the Knicks with a 24 point (10-14 shooting), 29 rebound, 4 assist, and 9 blocked shot game – despite playing with a broken hand! He was 35 years old.*

- In the 1973 Western Conference Finals Game 7 against the Chicago Bulls, the 36 year old Chamberlain topped off a 21 point, 28 rebound performance by blocking a shot with 30 seconds left and throwing a full-court pass for a layup that gave the Lakers the lead. They won 95-92.

Perhaps the best way to gauge a player's ability to rise to the occasion is to see how he performed when everything was on the line – in do-or-die situations where a loss meant the end of a season and a win meant survival or a ring. Wilt's performances in such games against the Boston Celtics are given above. Here is what he did against other teams:

<u>Do or Die games between Wilt and Teams
other than the Celtics</u>

1960 Game 3, Philadelphia vs. Syracuse – 132-112 Philly
     Wilt - 53 pts. (24/42 fg, 5/16 ft)   22 reb.   2 ass.

1961 Game 3, Philadelphia vs. Syracuse – 106-103 Syracuse
     Wilt - 33 pts. (13/29 fg, 7/14 ft)   23 reb.   1 ass.

1962 Game 5, Philadelphia vs. Syracuse – 121-104 Philly
     Wilt - 56 pts. (22/48 fg, 12/22 ft) 35 reb.   1 ass.

1964 Game 7, San Francisco vs. St. Louis – 105-95 SF
     Wilt - 39 pts. (19/29 fg, 1/6 ft)   30 reb.   6 ass.

1970 Game 5, Los Angeles vs. Phoenix – 138-121 Lakers
     Wilt - 36 pts. (12/20 fg, 12/19 ft)   14 reb.   3 ass.

1970 Game 6, Los Angeles vs. Phoenix – 104-93 Lakers
     Wilt - 12 pts. (4/11 fg, 4/12 ft)   26 reb. 11 ass.

1970 Game 7, Los Angeles vs. Phoenix – 129-94 Lakers
     Wilt - 30 pts. (11/18 fg, 8/17 ft)   27 reb.   6 ass.

1970 Game 6, Los Angeles vs. New York – 135-113 Lakers
     Wilt - 45 pts. (20/27 fg, 5/14 ft)   27 reb.   3 ass,

1970 Game 7, Los Angeles vs. New York – 113-99 Knicks
     Wilt - 21 pts. (10/16 fg, 1/11 ft)   24 reb.   4 ass.

1971 Game 7, Los Angeles vs. Chicago – 109-98 Lakers
     Wilt - 25 (7/12 fg, 11/17 ft)   19 reb.   9 ass.

1971 Game 5, Los Angeles vs. Milwaukee – 116-98 Bucks
     Wilt 23 pts. (10/21 fg, 3/9 ft)   12 reb.   4 ass.

1973 Game 7, Los Angeles vs. Chicago – 95-92 Lakers
     Wilt - 21 pts. (10/17 fg, 1/1 ft)   28 reb.   4 ass.

1973 Game 5, Los Angeles vs. New York – 102-93 Knicks
     Wilt - 23 pts. (9/16 – 5/14)   21 reb.   3 ass.

In 28 must-win playoff games (15 against Bill Russell and the Celtics and 13 against other opponents), Wilt's teams were 13-15 (4-11 against Boston, 9-4 against all others) and he compiled the following per game statistics:

FT	FTA	FT%	FG	FGA	FG%	PPG	RPG	APG
6.2	13.6	45.6%	11.3	21.3	53.1%	29.3	25.8	4.4

It escapes me how anyone can call a player who scores 29 points (on 53% shooting), grabs 26 rebounds, dishes out more than 4 assists, and blocks a bunch of shots in "win or go home games" a choker. But that's exactly what has happened all too often to Wilton Norman Chamberlain.

5. BUT NO ONE'S PERFECT

There's no denying it; Wilt was a very poor free throw shooter. His shooting percentage – 51.1% for his career - is almost 3% *lower* than his field goal percentage! Wilt tried everything, including shooting underhand and psychiatric therapy. He quipped that, at the end of his therapy sessions, the psychiatrist was a better free throw shooter than he was.

However, Bill Russell wasn't much better at this than Wilt (56.1% lifetime) and, as the years have gone by, it has become more and more apparent that big men tend to be challenged in this part of the game.

Other terrible free throw shooters include Shaquille O'Neal (52.7% career), Ben Wallace (41.4% career), Dwight Howard (currently 56.6% career), DeAndre Jordan (currently 45.1% career), and Andre Drummond (currently 42.4% career).

All of these are big, strong men. Celtic great Tom Heinsohn said that, in his opinion, superior strength can be a disability at the charity stripe. At a practice, he once watched Wilt make 20 out of 25 free throws *from half court!*

(This story makes one wonder how Chamberlain would have fared as a 3 point shooter. He was actually a good long range marksman when not standing still. His accurate hook shots and fall-away bank shots from 10-18 feet were unstoppable. There is a video of him making four long hook shots in a row during practice, the last one to win a $5 bet. Leading the league – or at least his position – in 3 point field goal percentage might have been a challenge Wilt couldn't resist.)

Heinsohn also noted that Wilt's famous fall-away jumper was effective because it minimized his overpowering strength and gave him more control over the ball. Be that as it may, subsequent NBA history and the continuing free throw struggles of big men have made Wilt's weakness in this area a tiny bit less shameful.

6. THE GOAT?

Harvey Pollack worked for the NBA for over 60 years, working most of that time as statistician for the Philadelphia 76ers. He said that Wilt Chamberlain was the greatest player he ever saw. Oscar Robertson and Earl "the Pearl" Monroe have said without hesitation that Wilt was the GOAT, and they both played against him. Larry Bird and Oscar said that the record book proved Wilt was the GOAT.

In Larry's words:

Let me tell you something. For a while, they were saying that I was the greatest. And before me, it was Magic who was the greatest. And then it's Michael's [Jordan] turn. But open up the record book and it will be obvious who the greatest is.

Bill Russell had this to say:

If Wilt were playing today, he would be even more dominant than he was then. I don't see a center out there now that could play against him. The reason people don't believe that is because Wilt's numbers were so big, they seemed so impossible that they almost don't seem real. So they try to find a way to dismiss them or devalue them and try to make them not real.

Nobody seems to appreciate what an incredible player Wilt was. He was the best player of all time because he dominated the floor like nobody else ever could. To be that big and that athletic was special.

Generally speaking, players will name the greatest player of their generation as the greatest player of all time - to prove that they did whatever they did against the absolute best. If pride forbids that, then they will name the greatest player of the generation immediately before them – the player they grew up idolizing and emulating.

I've never heard a player name himself as the greatest of all time, except for Wilt Chamberlain, though he did so with a grin and a twinkle in his eye. And he also named Bill Russell as the greatest center ever because he believed that Bill fit into the team concept better than he did.

When asked in a 1997 interview with Ahmad Rashad to name his all-time top five players – not including himself and Bill Russell - Wilt replied with seven names:

> *Okay, well, Larry Bird and, ah, let's see... Larry Bird and I gotta go with Jerry [West], Oscar [Robertson], and Elgin [Baylor] and, ah, probably Jordan or Magic. Six, can you give me six? Can I have seven and put Sir Charles [Barkley] in there? Sir Charles is my favorite choice.*

There have been several outstanding basketball players who have been put forward as the greatest of their time, or of all time. My short list, in no particular order, is Bill Russell, Jerry West, Oscar Robertson, Kareem Abdul-Jabbar, Larry Bird, Magic Johnson, Hakeem Olajuwon, George Mikan, Lebron James, Michael Jordan, Shaquille O'Neal, and Elgin Baylor.

However, none of them came close to possessing the same range of physical skills that Wilt Chamberlain had. His combination of speed, strength, stamina, athletic ability, and versatility was unmatched – even unapproached.

As may be evident in the preceding pages, strong cases can be made that Wilt was the greatest scorer, rebounder, shot blocker, playmaker (at his position), and most durable player in NBA history. That can't be claimed for anyone else.

At age 36, after knee surgery that severely limited his lateral mobility, Wilt led the league in rebounding, field goal percentage, and (if official records had been kept) shot-blocking. In my opinion, no player was more dominant, more revolutionary, or more unfairly maligned than Wilt Chamberlain.

That said, I think it is impossible to give an objective answer to the GOAT question. There are far too many variables within a player's game: his various skills, weaknesses (everybody has them), physical, mental, and emotional makeup and how well he works with this teammates, the quality of coaching he receives, how well he fits into his team(s) and even his conference, and how his game evolves over time.

Some players excel at the highest level for a short period of time before injuries or other factors reduce their effectiveness (consider Bill Walton, Grant Hill, Mark Price, David Thompson, Tracy McGrady). Other players have limited roles because of their physiques, teammates, or other factors, but are unsurpassed at what they do best (consider George Gervin, Wes Unseld, Allen Iverson, Tiny Archibald, John Stockton, Dennis Rodman, Mark Eaton).

And then there is the impossibility of comparing players from different eras, with different game rules, training methods, levels of competition, styles of play, past examples to emulate and learn from, travel and accommodations, and on and on.

In my opinion, comparing basketball players is like comparing leaders in other fields. Consider the following – how would you rank these in order of greatness?

> **Painters:** Leonardo Da Vinci, Pablo Picasso, Gustav Klimt, Johannes Vermeer, Rembrandt, Salvador Dali, Hieronymus Bosch, Raphael, Jean-Michel Basquiat
>
> **Guitarists:** Charlie Christian, Django Rheinhardt, Chuck Berry, George Harrison, Eric Clapton, Jimmy Page, Jimi Hendrix, Les Paul, Duane Allman, Eddie Van Halen
>
> **Generals:** Hannibal, Julius Caesar, Robert E. Lee, Genghis Khan, Alexander the Great, Norman Schwarzkopf, Erwin Rommel, George S. Patton, U. S. Grant, Napoleon, Dwight Eisenhower
>
> **Writers:** William Shakespeare, Dante Alighieri, James Joyce, Charles Dickens, Mark Twain, Jane Austen, Emily Bronte, Stephen King, Ernest Hemingway

I haven't said much so far about accolades such as MVP awards, All-NBA team selections, All-Star recognition. That is because I don't take these subjective nods any more seriously than I do Oscars, Emmys, or Tonys.

Wilt received quite a few of these (e.g. 4 MVPs), but, in my opinion not nearly as many as he deserved. The winners reflect the prejudices and preferences of the voters, who reflect the politics and marketing strategy of the NBA. Truth is, I've disagreed with a high percentage of the awards during the 50-plus years I've been following the NBA, so I have learned to take them with plenty of salt and I certainly don't take them as "proof" of greatness or as statistics for player comparisons.

Bill Russell once averaged 20 points and 20 rebounds for the national champion University of San Francisco team – but was not named the best center *in his own conference*. And in 1961-62, Wilt Chamberlain averaged 50 points and 25 rebounds, led the league in points, rebounds, win shares, and minutes played, was second in field goal percentage, and took his team to within 2 points of dethroning the champion Boston Celtics in a seven game semifinal series - and yet came in a distant second to Bill Russell in MVP voting. Apparently, not enough people loved Goliath that year.

Wilt himself gave away all of the awards he received during his storied career – except for his Hall of Fame citation. He claimed that the trophies made other people happier than they made him.

Time passes, records are broken – even Wilt's – and the game changes. The fan of the modern game may struggle to appreciate the game of Wilt's era. The players look awkward in film, slowed down by hand-checking, no palming of the ball, and frequent charging calls at a time when slam dunks were considered showing off and inappropriate for all but the giants. And it was a time when overtly taunting opponents or preening after a play were almost unthinkable.

The day will probably come when the present-day style will

look antiquated and awkward, and some fools may even say that Steph Curry and Lebron James would be benchwarmers in the future.

However, some players will be remembered as having been above and beyond the standards of their time. They will become legends and heroes for all time, admired and respected by almost everyone, their weaknesses all but forgotten as their greatness shines forth to inspire and awe future generations.

I am writing of people like Babe Ruth, Jackie Robinson, Mickey Mantle, Ted Williams, Willie Mays, and Hank Aaron in baseball; Muhammad Ali, Joe Louis, Jack Johnson, and Rocky Marciano in boxing; Wayne Gretzky, Gordie Howe, and Bobby Orr in hockey; Arnold Palmer, Jack Nicklaus, and Tiger Woods in golf; Pelé and Maradona in soccer; Jim Brown, Jim Thorpe, and Joe Montana in football; Bill Russell, Larry Bird, and Michael Jordan in basketball.

I believe that Wilt Chamberlain belongs in this category without any "asterisks."

7. ROSEBUD

Wilt wasn't as brash as Muhammad Ali in declaring his greatness. But being recognized as the GOAT was clearly very important to him.

When one reads about the sad final months of Wilt's life, alone most of the time in his mountain-top mansion in the Belair section of Los Angeles, his physical powers gone, barely able to climb his own stairs, one is reminded of Charles Foster Kane in Orson Welles' classic film, "Citizen Kane." Kane is haunted by the one thing he could never recapture, represented by his last word "Rosebud," which stood for the lost happiness of childhood.

If Wilt had a "Rosebud," it may have been public recognition that he was the greatest basketball player of all time. He probably felt that he had earned the GOAT title, by writing the record book, by sacrificing his game for his team, by outplaying everyone in his generation – and then by holding his own against the best of the next generation (Kareem).

It must have galled him to see Bill Russell selected as the greatest player of the first half century of the NBA, then to watch as Kareem Abdul-Jabbar surpassed his career scoring record, then to see Michael Jordan become the consensus GOAT – even to read that Dennis Rodman was supposedly the greatest rebounder of all time.

In 1997, when Wilt was honored as one of the 50 greatest players in NBA history at the All-Star game, he sat in front of another great, Clyde Drexler. Drexler was asked by broadcaster Craig Sager what his favorite autograph from the event was. Drexler replied "Well, the greatest of all times! He's right here in front of me..."

Wilt turned around beaming and pretended to pass money to Clyde. Sager asked Chamberlain how many points he would score in 1997 and, with his customary modesty, after explaining how the rule changes would favor him, Wilt replied "Probably 65 or 70."

On the same occasion, Wilt met Michael Jordan, probably his greatest rival for the GOAT title, for the first time. Bill Walton, another of the "50 Greatest," described what happened:

> *We're at the NBA's All-Time team celebration in Cleveland in 1997, and over in the corner is Wilt and Michael Jordan. And they're sitting at a table arguing vociferously as to who the greatest player of all time is. And they're back and forth, and they're just intent as can be.*
>
> *And so now David Stern [NBA Commissioner] comes into the room and he says "Okay guys, time to go." And Michael and Wilt are still going at it at this table over here. And so David finally says "Come on Wilt, Michael. We gotta get going!"*
>
> *And so they stand up and Wilt, who always has the last word in everything; Wilt looked down at Michael and said "Michael, just remember. When you played, they changed all the rules to make it easier for you to dominate. When I played, they changed all the rules to make it harder for me." And there was no retort, no comeback. Wilt Chamberlain. Oh my gosh!*

During a television interview at about the same time, Wilt confronted an interviewer who favored MJ:

> *I mean, listen, I know that basketball is a team game, and you've already made Michael number one, but if you had to have Wilt against Michael, my prime, his prime, how much money would you be willing to bet?*

The audience oohed and aahed.

We might get a hint of what would have happened from a televised, post-career one-on-one matchup between Julius Erving and Kareem Abdul-Jabbar. Kareem won and it wasn't close. An agile big man with an outside shooting touch - like Wilt and Kareem - has a huge advantage.

Wilt never tired of trying to be understood, of explaining without actually coming out and saying it why he should be considered the GOAT. He wrote three books that, if you read between the lines, were intended to make his case, both by reminding people of his accomplishments and by casting doubt on the arguments for his rivals.

Near the very end of his life, he attended a celebration of Bill Russell in Boston. He was the butt of stories that illustrated Russell's greatness and accomplishments. Then, after watching an HBO documentary that burnished Russell's legend, Wilt called the famous sportswriter Frank Deford aside. To quote Deford from his 2012 *Sports Illustrated* article entitled "When the NBA Was Young":

> *Wilt looked enviously at Russell. There he was, after all these years, the conquering hero once again. Wilt then turned back to me. "You think you could do me a favor?" he asked, almost sheepishly.*
>
> *"Sure. What is it?"*
>
> *"You think you can do one of those HBO things on me that you did on Bill?"*
>
> *"Sure," I said. I was pretty certain HBO would be delighted.*
>
> *"I could really use that," Wilt said—and maybe for the first time I realized how beaten down he had been, how much he'd been mocked for the 20,000-women claim. Neither of us knew, of course, that by October of that year, before the HBO special could be shot, Wilt would be dead at only 63.*
>
> *"I'll give you a call," I said.*
>
> *"Thanks, Frank. I'd appreciate that."*

I can almost hear Wilt looking over my shoulder right now, whispering "Come on, say it. Say I was the greatest basketball player of all time."

Well, Big Dipper, the records speak for themselves, don't they?

8. NBA STATS & GAME LOGS

Ultimately, it doesn't really matter what people say about Wilt Chamberlain as a basketball player. What matters is what he did on the court. Accordingly, the following pages present the record of what this man did, asterisks aside. There are some gaps and omissions, but these are as complete as I could make them. Read and wonder.

As mentioned previously, the blocked shot statistics are unofficial. They come from a variety of news sources, including newspaper accounts, game footage, and coaching staff records.

For more about the great Wilt Chamberlain, I suggest looking up his interviews on YouTube and, for game footage and more, checking out the *Wilt Chamberlain Archive*, also on YouTube. Prepare to be charmed by the former and awed by the latter.

Also, I highly recommend the following books, three of them by Wilt himself:

Chamberlain, Wilt, *Wilt: Just Like Any Other 7-Foot Black Millionaire Who Lives Next Door*, MacMillan, New York, 1973.

Chamberlain, Wilt, *A View From Above*, Villard Books, New York, 1991.

Chamberlain, Wilt, *Who's Running the Asylum? Inside the Insane World of Sports Today*, ProMotion Publishing, San Diego, 1997.

Cherry, Robert, *Wilt: Larger than Life*, Triumph Books, 2004.

Pomerantz, Gary M., *Wilt, 1962*, Crown Publishers, New York, 2005.

Season	Tm	G	MP	FG	FGA	FG%	FT	FTA	FT%	TRB	AST	PF	PTS
1959-60	PHW	72	46.4	15.0	32.1	0.461	8.0	13.8	0.582	27.0	2.3	2.1	37.6
1960-61	PHW	79	47.8	16.0	31.1	0.509	6.7	13.3	0.504	27.2	1.9	1.6	38.4
1961-62	PHW	80	48.5	20.0	39.5	0.506	10.0	17.0	0.613	25.7	2.4	1.5	50.4
1962-63	SFW	80	47.6	18.0	34.6	0.528	8.3	13.9	0.593	24.3	3.4	1.7	44.8
1963-64	SFW	80	46.1	15.0	28.7	0.524	6.8	12.7	0.531	22.3	5.0	2.3	36.9
1964-65	TOT	73	45.2	15.0	28.5	0.510	5.6	12.1	0.464	22.9	3.4	2.0	34.7
1964-65	SFW	38	45.9	17.0	33.6	0.499	5.5	13.2	0.416	23.5	3.1	2.0	38.9
1964-65	PHI	35	44.5	12.0	23.1	0.528	5.7	10.9	0.526	22.3	3.8	2.0	30.1
1965-66	PHI	79	47.3	14.0	25.2	0.540	6.3	12.4	0.513	24.6	5.2	2.2	33.5
1966-67	PHI	81	45.5	9.7	14.2	0.683	4.8	10.8	0.441	24.2	7.8	1.8	24.1
1967-68	PHI	82	46.8	10.0	16.8	0.595	4.3	11.4	0.380	23.8	8.6	2.0	24.3
1968-69	LAL	81	45.3	7.9	13.6	0.583	4.7	10.6	0.446	21.1	4.5	1.8	20.5
1969-70	LAL	12	42.1	11.0	18.9	0.568	5.8	13.1	0.446	18.4	4.1	2.6	27.3
1970-71	LAL	82	44.3	8.1	15.0	0.545	4.4	8.2	0.538	18.2	4.3	2.1	20.7
1971-72	LAL	82	42.3	6.0	9.3	0.649	2.7	6.4	0.422	19.2	4.0	2.4	14.8
1972-73	LAL	82	43.2	5.2	7.1	0.727	2.8	5.5	0.510	18.6	4.5	2.3	13.2
Career		**1045**	**45.8**	**12.0**	**22.5**	**0.540**	**5.8**	**11.4**	**0.511**	**22.9**	**4.4**	**2.0**	**30.1**

PHW = Philadephia Warriors   SFW = San Francisco Warriors   PHI - Phildelphia 76ers   LAL = Los Angeles Lakers

CAREER PLAYOFF Averages

Season	Tm	G	MP	FG	FGA	FG%	FT	FTA	FT%	TRB	AST	PF	PTS
1959-60	PHW	9	46.1	14.0	28.0	0.496	5.4	12.2	0.445	25.8	2.1	1.9	33.2
1960-61	PHW	3	48.0	15.0	32.0	0.469	7.0	12.7	0.553	23.0	2.0	3.3	37.0
1961-62	PHW	12	48.0	14.0	28.9	0.467	8.0	12.6	0.636	26.6	3.1	2.3	35.0
1963-64	SFW	12	46.5	15.0	26.8	0.543	5.5	11.6	0.475	25.2	3.3	2.3	34.7
1964-65	PHI	11	48.7	11.0	21.1	0.530	6.9	12.4	0.559	27.2	4.4	2.6	29.3
1965-66	PHI	5	48.0	11.0	22.0	0.509	5.6	13.6	0.412	30.2	3.0	2.0	28.0
1966-67	PHI	15	47.9	8.8	15.2	0.579	4.1	10.7	0.388	29.1	9.0	2.5	21.7
1967-68	PHI	13	48.5	9.5	17.8	0.534	4.6	12.2	0.380	24.7	6.5	2.2	23.7
1968-69	LAL	18	46.2	5.3	9.8	0.545	3.2	8.2	0.392	24.7	2.6	3.1	13.9
1969-70	LAL	18	47.3	8.8	16.0	0.549	4.6	11.2	0.406	22.2	4.5	2.3	22.1
1970-71	LAL	12	46.2	7.1	15.6	0.455	4.2	8.1	0.515	20.2	4.4	2.8	18.3
1971-72	LAL	15	46.9	5.3	9.5	0.563	4.0	8.1	0.492	21.0	3.3	3.1	14.7
1972-73	LAL	17	47.1	3.8	6.8	0.552	2.9	5.8	0.500	22.5	3.5	2.8	10.4
Career		**160**	**47.2**	**8.9**	**17.1**	**0.522**	**4.7**	**10.2**	**0.465**	**24.5**	**4.2**	**2.6**	**22.5**

PHW = Philadephia Warriors   SFW = San Francisco Warriors   PHI - Phildelphia 76ers   LAL = Los Angeles Lakers

G	Date	Opp	W/L	MP	FG	FGA	FG%	FT	FTA	FT%	TRB	AST	BLK	PF	PTS
1	10/24/1959	NYK	W (+9)	48	17	27	0.630	9	15	0.600	28	1		4	43
2	10/31/1959	DET	W (+8)	47	13	32	0.406	10	15	0.667	34	2		0	36
3	11/4/1959	SYR	W (+11)	47	17	40	0.425	7	15	0.467	40	0		1	41
4	11/7/1959	BOS	L (-9)	48	12	38	0.316	6	12	0.500	28	1		2	30
5	11/8/1959	CIN	W (+28)	39	12	32	0.375	8	14	0.571	35	2		0	32
6	11/10/1959	NYK	W (+1)	48	14	29	0.483	11	19	0.579	43	4		3	39
7	11/11/1959	DET	W (+14)	48	16	34	0.471	9	12	0.75	17	1		3	41
8	11/12/1959	CIN	W (+8)	47	23	43	0.535	9	16	0.563	29	2		3	55
9	11/14/1959	MNL	W (+6)	48	10	35	0.286	8	14	0.571	33	0		0	28
10	11/15/1959	MNL	L (-6)	48	11	29	0.379	4	9	0.444	25	2		1	26
11	11/20/1959	STL	L (-1)	48	9	28	0.321	6	9	0.667	28	4		5	24
12	11/21/1959	SYR	L (-9)	45	9	26	0.346	10	14	0.714	26	1		2	28
13	11/22/1959	SYR	W (+11)	48	15	32	0.469	7	11	0.636	24	2		0	37
14	11/25/1959	BOS	W (+10)	48	19	37	0.514	7	16	0.438	35	1	6	4	45
15	11/26/1959	BOS	W (+13)	48	19	33	0.576	11	16	0.688	33	2		1	49
16	11/28/1959	NYK	W (+1)	48	11	29	0.379	6	10	0.600	21	2		2	28
17	11/29/1959	NYK	L (-1)	48	12	32	0.375	9	13	0.692	34	4		1	33
18	12/3/1959	MNL	W (+14)	48	15	29	0.517	11	12	0.917	33	1		1	41
19	12/4/1959	STL	W (+12)	43	14	26	0.538	11	17	0.647	25	1		3	39
20	12/5/1959	STL	L (-1)	48	6	19	0.316	8	15	0.533	20	1		4	20
21	12/9/1959	BOS	L (-21)	43	14	31	0.452	11	19	0.579	20	0		2	39

G	Date	Opp	W/L	MP	FG	FGA	FG%	FT	FTA	FT%	TRB	AST	BLK	PF	PTS
22	12/10/1959	CIN	W (+19)	33	13	32	0.406	8	9	0.889	22	0		2	34
23	12/12/1959	BOS	L (-9)	48	6	17	0.353	10	19	0.526	25	1		3	22
24	12/13/1959	SYR	L (-29)	35	14	29	0.483	8	11	0.727	15	0		1	36
25	12/15/1959	CIN	W (+24)	47	16	32	0.500	6	11	0.545	18	2		3	38
26	12/16/1959	CIN	W (+9)	48	16	29	0.552	11	19	0.579	24	1		1	43
27	12/19/1959	STL	L (-13)	48	9	26	0.346	12	15	0.800	21	1		4	30
28	12/25/1959	SYR	W (+8)		15	33	0.455	15	24	0.625	34	2		0	45
29	12/26/1959	NYK	L (-6)	48	13	34	0.382	13	21	0.619	31	1		3	39
30	12/28/1959	CIN	W (+5)	47	14	33	0.424	11	18	0.611	39	3		0	39
31	12/30/1959	MNL	W (+15)	46	19	51	0.373	7	11	0.636	32	3		3	45
32	1/2/1960	BOS	W (+1)	48	18	36	0.500	11	14	0.786	36	1		2	47
33	1/5/1960	MNL	W (+15)	48	20	38	0.526	12	18	0.667	20	0	10	3	52
34	1/6/1960	STL	W (+20)	45	11	23	0.478	5	10	0.500	19	1		3	27
35	1/7/1960	DET	W (+15)	46	16	24	0.667	12	20	0.600	30	1		3	44
36	1/9/1960	SYR	W (+7)	48	20	38	0.526	8	15	0.533	37	3		3	48
37	1/10/1960	NYK	W (+13)	48	13	42	0.310	9	13	0.692	27	7		2	35
38	1/12/1960	STL	W (+18)	46	13	25	0.520	11	18	0.611	22	3		3	37
39	1/13/1960	SYR	W (+1)	53	15	32	0.469	12	21	0.571	39	5		1	42
40	1/15/1960	BOS	L (-12)	48	16	42	0.381	12	19	0.632	43	2		2	44
41	1/17/1960	BOS	L (-6)	48	19	34	0.559	5	17	0.294	26	1		2	43
42	1/19/1960	NYK	W (+21)	45	14	35	0.400	2	9	0.222	23	4		2	30

G	Date	Opp	W/L	MP	FG	FGA	FG%	FT	FTA	FT%	TRB	AST	BLK	PF	PTS
43	1/20/1960	SYR	W (+6)	47	12	27	0.444	9	21	0.429	31	5		5	33
44	1/23/1960	DET	L (-20)	46	16	36	0.444	12	25	0.48	25	2		1	44
45	1/24/1960	CIN	W (+9)	48	10	31	0.323	10	18	0.556	37	6		2	30
46	1/25/1960	DET	W (+10)	47	24	41	0.585	10	13	0.769	42	4		3	58
47	1/27/1960	NYK	W (+12)	47	19	37	0.514	5	6	0.833	21	5		1	43
48	1/29/1960	BOS	W (+8)	48	18	36	0.500	7	15	0.467	39	3		2	43
49	1/30/1960	NYK	L (-7)	48	22	39	0.564	1	4	0.250	21	3		2	45
50	1/31/1960	MNL	W (+10)	48	15	35	0.429	11	16	0.688	33	1		3	41
51	2/1/1960	MNL	W (+7)	47	10	23	0.435	3	12	0.250	28	5		2	23
52	2/2/1960	CIN	W (+2)	47	13	22	0.591	8	13	0.615	27	4		1	34
53	2/4/1960	SYR	L (-27)	48	18	36	0.500	7	13	0.538	24	4		2	43
54	2/6/1960	SYR	W (+3)	48	15	37	0.405	14	23	0.609	45	3		2	44
55	2/7/1960	STL	L (-22)	48	13	29	0.448	12	20	0.600	20	5		3	38
56	2/9/1960	DET	L (-9)	48	19	37	0.514	3	5	0.600	17	4		3	41
57	2/10/1960	NYK	L (-8)	9:00	2	5	0.400	1	2	0.500	2	1		0	5
58	2/14/1960	BOS	L (-10)	41	10	21	0.476	5	11	0.455	19	2		0	25
59	2/16/1960	CIN	W (+5)	47	16	28	0.571	12	18	0.667	30	1		4	44
60	2/17/1960	SYR	W (+7)	46	12	29	0.414	9	15	0.600	25	3		3	33
61	2/18/1960	SYR	L (-14)	48	15	33	0.455	3	7	0.429	19	4		1	33
62	2/20/1960	MNL	W (+16)	46	17	32	0.531	7	14	0.500	20	3		3	41
63	2/21/1960	NYK	W (+7)	48	26	47	0.553	6	9	0.667	24	3		1	58

G	Date	Opp	W/L	MP	FG	FGA	FG%	FT	FTA	FT%	TRB	AST	BLK	PF	PTS
64	2/23/1960	BOS	W (+18)	47	25	44	0.568	3	11	0.273	29	1	11	2	53
65	2/25/1960	NYK	W (+10)	48	18	33	0.545	3	7	0.429	22	2		3	39
66	2/27/1960	MNL	L (-18)	48	12	28	0.429	10	16	0.625	22	1		2	34
67	2/28/1960	DET	W (+2)	48	10	25	0.400	3	12	0.250	15	2		1	23
68	3/2/1960	BOS	L (-14)	48	16	36	0.444	7	10	0.700	25	1	14	2	39
69	3/3/1960	DET	W (+9)	47	18	38	0.474	5	7	0.714	19	3		3	41
70	3/4/1960	NYK	W (+2)	53	19	39	0.487	4	8	0.500	22	0		1	42
71	3/6/1960	STL	L (-19)	48	13	28	0.464	6	10	0.600	20	3		2	32
72	3/9/1960	SYR	L (-11)	48	14	33	0.424	3	5	0.600	24	2		5	31

1960 Playoffs

1	3/11/1960	SYR	W (+23)	48	16	36	0.440	3	10	0.300	27	3	2	35
2	3/13/1960	SYR	L (-6)	48	11	26	0.420	6	9	0.667	18	2	2	28
3	3/14/1960	SYR	W (+20)	47	24	42	0.570	5	16	0.313	22	2	0	53
4	3/16/1960	BOS	L (-6)	48	17	35	0.490	8	14	0.571	29	1	2	42
5	3/18/1960	BOS	W (+5)	48	12	23	0.520	5	10	0.500	28	1	1	29
6	3/19/1960	BOS	L (-30)	35	6	13	0.460	0	6	0.000	15	6	1	12
7	3/20/1960	BOS	L (-8)	48	9	17	0.530	6	11	0.545	34	2	2	24
8	3/22/1960	BOS	W (+21)	46	22	42	0.520	6	14	0.429	35	2	2	50
9	3/24/1960	BOS	L (-2)	48	8	18	0.440	10	16	0.625	24	0	5	26

G	Date	Opp	W/L	MP	FG	FGA	FG%	FT	FTA	FT%	TRB	AST	BLK	PF	PTS
1	10/22/1960	SYR	W (+10)	47	18	35	0.514	6	15	0.400	31	1		1	42
2	10/28/1960	LAL	W (+2)	48	14	35	0.400	1	6	0.167	23	1		4	29
3	10/29/1960	BOS	W (+28)	44	12	29	0.414	2	8	0.250	27	1		3	26
4	11/1/1960	CIN	W (+18)	47	14	34	0.412	5	11	0.455	25		9	0	33
5	11/4/1960	DET	W (+15)	47	22	35	0.629	0	10	0.000	39	3	12	2	44
6	11/5/1960	DET	W (+7)	48	13	39	0.333	6	8	0.750	26	2		2	32
7	11/9/1960	LAL	W (+7)	48	20	36	0.556	6	16	0.375	27	1		1	46
8	11/10/1960	NYK	W (+4)	53	9	29	0.310	4	12	0.333	30	6	10	0	22
9	11/11/1960	STL	W (+5)	48	14	27	0.519	9	15	0.600	35	3		4	37
10	11/12/1960	STL	L (-2)	48	18	33	0.545	6	12	0.500	24	0		2	42
11	11/15/1960	CIN	L (-9)	48	16	29	0.552	4	11	0.364	29	2		1	36
12	11/16/1960	DET	L (-1)	48	18	30	0.600	5	13	0.385	22	0		1	41
13	11/17/1960	SYR	L (-1)	48	18	39	0.462	9	27	0.333	28	1		1	45
14	11/18/1960	NYK	W (+2)	48	14	29	0.483	6	15	0.400	23	3		2	34
15	11/19/1960	NYK	W (+10)	44	16	27	0.593	8	13	0.615	28	0		0	40
16	11/24/1960	BOS	L (-3)	48	15	42	0.357	4	10	0.400	55	4	8	3	34
17	11/26/1960	CIN	W (+30)	44	18	33	0.545	10	19	0.526	16	2		1	46
18	11/27/1960	LAL	W (+7)	48	16	48	0.333	9	17	0.529	27			3	41
19	11/28/1960	LAL	L (-25)	48	19	34	0.559	5	11	0.455	18	1		1	43
20	11/29/1960	LAL	W (+1)	48	21	45	0.467	2	8	0.250	38	7		1	44
21	12/1/1960	LAL	W (+3)	48	19	38	0.500	3	11	0.273	23	2		1	41

G	Date	Opp	W/L	MP	FG	FGA	FG%	FT	FTA	FT%	TRB	AST	BLK	PF	PTS
22	12/3/1960	STL	L (-4)	48	13	23	0.565	9	16	0.563	25	1		4	35
23	12/6/1960	SYR	W (+6)	48	15	32	0.469	1	7	0.143	22	2		2	31
24	12/8/1960	NYK	W (+3)	48	17	35	0.486	12	21	0.571	29	1		2	46
25	12/10/1960	BOS	W (+5)	48	14	32	0.438	6	10	0.600	30	1		1	34
26	12/11/1960	SYR	L (-11)	46	12	26	0.462	7	10	0.700	27	1		2	31
27	12/13/1960	DET	W (+2)	48	17	23	0.739	2	6	0.333	18	0		2	36
28	12/14/1960	DET	L (-8)	47	9	28	0.321	12	16	0.750	20	3		3	30
29	12/16/1960	STL	L (-5)	48	15	31	0.484	4	7	0.571	25	1		0	34
30	12/18/1960	CIN	W (+16)	40	14	31	0.452	4	9	0.444	38	3		0	32
31	12/21/1960	NYK	W (+5)	48	14	31	0.452	5	9	0.556	26	2		0	33
32	12/26/1960	BOS	L (-4)	48	12	31	0.387	6	15	0.400	36	2		2	30
33	12/27/1960	BOS	W (+15)	47	14	33	0.424	11	17	0.647	30	2		2	39
34	12/29/1960	CIN	W (+4)	48	11	20	0.550	5	14	0.357	26	3		2	27
35	12/30/1960	CIN	L (-6)	48	20	33	0.606	9	14	0.643	24	1		2	49
36	1/2/1961	NYK	W (+16)	48	23	37	0.622	10	20	0.500	28	0		2	56
37	1/3/1961	DET	W (+3)	53	17	34	0.500	12	20	0.600	33	6		3	46
38	1/5/1961	SYR	W (+12)	48	20	32	0.625	16	22	0.727	26	1		1	56
39	1/8/1961	NYK	L (-2)	48	16	32	0.500	6	14	0.429	31	2		3	38
40	1/12/1961	STL	W (+9)	48	16	30	0.533	5	10	0.500	32	2		1	37
41	1/13/1961	BOS	L (-2)	53	12	28	0.429	6	18	0.333	35	1		3	30
42	1/14/1961	BOS	W (+3)	48	17	27	0.630	10	18	0.556	35	1		3	44

G	Date	Opp	W/L	MP	FG	FGA	FG%	FT	FTA	FT%	TRB	AST	BLK	PF	PTS
43	1/15/1961	SYR	L (-3)	48	8	20	0.400	8	15	0.533	22	1		2	24
44	1/18/1961	SYR	L (-11)	48	17	36	0.472	14	21	0.667	18	1		2	48
45	1/19/1961	STL	W (+2)	48	16	31	0.516	7	16	0.438	28	1		3	39
46	1/21/1961	LAL	W (+25)	48	25	46	0.543	6	13	0.462	45	0		2	56
47	1/22/1961	DET	L (-8)	48	11	23	0.478	6	12	0.5	24	4		2	28
48	1/24/1961	STL	L (-2)	48	6	14	0.429	4	9	0.444	36	5		0	16
49	1/26/1961	BOS	L (-8)	48	10	18	0.556	5	8	0.625	24	2		0	25
50	1/27/1961	NYK	L (-11)	48	8	15	0.533	8	14	0.571	16	2		2	24
51	1/28/1961	NYK	W (+6)	48	11	33	0.333	6	13	0.462	18	3		3	28
52	1/29/1961	BOS	L (-13)	48	19	29	0.655	8	14	0.571	20	1		0	46
53	2/1/1961	SYR	W (+9)	48	13	32	0.406	4	9	0.444	29	0		2	30
54	2/2/1961	CIN	W (+15)	48	20	33	0.606	5	10	0.5	22	1		0	45
55	2/3/1961	CIN	W (+1)	48	23	38	0.605	6	11	0.545	30	0		1	52
56	2/5/1961	NYK	W (+8)	53	21	34	0.618	13	18	0.722	29	1	8+	4	55
57	2/7/1961	STL	L (-3)	48	13	34	0.382	11	20	0.55	21	2		2	37
58	2/8/1961	DET	L (-2)	48	18	34	0.529	6	16	0.375	19	1		1	42
59	2/9/1961	SYR	L (-10)	48	19	33	0.576	8	16	0.5	29	0		3	46
60	2/10/1961	NYK	W (+2)	48	21	33	0.636	6	14	0.429	36	3		3	48
61	2/12/1961	BOS	L (-11)	48	20	34	0.588	6	16	0.375	25	2		2	46
62	2/15/1961	STL	L (-37)	48	11	25	0.440	6	11	0.545	28	1		4	28
63	2/16/1961	BOS	W (+10)	48	15	23	0.652	4	6	0.667	28	4		2	34

G	Date	Opp	W/L	MP	FG	FGA	FG%	FT	FTA	FT%	TRB	AST	BLK	PF	PTS
64	2/17/1961	BOS	L (-5)	48	11	23	0.478	5	9	0.556	27	1		3	27
65	2/18/1961	SYR	L (-19)	48	9	25	0.360	12	17	0.706	17	2		1	30
66	2/21/1961	NYK	W (+2)	48	16	27	0.593	7	14	0.5	30	5		3	39
67	2/22/1961	CIN	W (+1)	48	16	25	0.640	9	16	0.563	22	1		1	41
68	2/23/1961	DET	W (+8)	48	22	38	0.579	5	10	0.500	28	1		2	49
69	2/25/1961	CIN	W (+9)	48	25	38	0.658	8	18	0.444	27			0	58
70	2/26/1961	LAL	L (-5)	48	15	26	0.577	4	8	0.500	26	1		0	34
71	2/27/1961	LAL	W (+25)	48	16	23	0.696	3	8	0.375	29	1		1	35
72	2/28/1961	LAL	W (+15)	48	14	33	0.424	4	11	0.364	31	1		0	32
73	3/1/1961	SYR	L (-21)	48	22	44	0.500	12	20	0.600	20	5		0	56
74	3/3/1961	SYR	W (+7)	48	17	42	0.405	13	17	0.765	27	2		2	47
75	3/4/1961	SYR	W (+1)	48	13	31	0.419	7	19	0.368	21	1		0	33
76	3/5/1961	BOS	L (-17)	48	20	39	0.513	7	12	0.583	26	2		2	47
77	3/9/1961	NYK	W (+9)	48	27	37	0.730	13	17	0.765	31	1		1	67
78	3/10/1961	DET	L (-17)	48	14	26	0.538	4	5	0.800	35	2		0	32
79	3/11/1961	STL	L (-43)	37	7	12	0.583	3	10	0.3	15	1		0	17

1961 Playoffs

G	Date	Opp	W/L	MP	FG	FGA	FG%	FT	FTA	FT%	TRB	AST	BLK	PF	PTS
1	3/14/1961	SYR	L (-8)	48	19	39	0.487	8	14	0.571	32	2		3	46
2	3/16/1961	SYR	L (-1)	48	13	28	0.464	6	10	0.600	14	3		4	32
3	3/18/1961	SYR	L (-3)	48	13	29	0.448	7	14	0.500	23	1		3	33

G	Date	Opp	W/L	MP	FG	FGA	FG%	FT	FTA	FT%	TRB	AST	BLK	PF	PTS
1	10/19/1961	LAL	L (-5)	48	21	44	0.477	6	12	0.500	25	1		1	48
2	10/20/1961	LAL	W (+7)	48	24	46	0.522	9	17	0.529	32	1		2	57
3	10/21/1961	NYK	W (+37)	48	21	41	0.512	11	17	0.647	35	2		0	53
4	10/27/1961	SYR	L (-4)	48	21	45	0.467	13	21	0.619	24	3		3	55
5	10/28/1961	SYR	W (+4)	48	17	43	0.395	9	14	0.643	23	3		0	43
6	11/3/1961	BOS	L (-14)	48	12	31	0.387	4	9	0.444	33	1		2	28
7	11/4/1961	DET	W (+3)	48	24	48	0.500	10	16	0.625	33	0		1	58
8	11/8/1961	DET	W (+4)	48	23	46	0.500	12	19	0.632	23	1		3	58
9	11/9/1961	SYR	W (+43)	48	20	38	0.526	15	27	0.556	29	0		1	55
10	11/11/1961	BOS	L (-3)	48	17	40	0.425	7	13	0.538	21	3		4	41
11	11/14/1961	NYK	L (-2)	48	13	27	0.481	8	17	0.471	18	2		2	34
12	11/15/1961	CIN	W (+12)	48	18	42	0.429	7	13	0.538	18	5		1	43
13	11/17/1961	LAL	L (-4)	48	24	48	0.500	8	19	0.421	32	2		1	56
14	11/18/1961	SYR	L (-18)	48	13	32	0.406	13	20	0.650	17	2		1	39
15	11/19/1961	CHP	W (+8)	48	24	47	0.511	3	8	0.375	16	0	9+	2	51
16	11/21/1961	CIN	W (+7)	48	20	44	0.455	5	15	0.333	34	6		0	45
17	11/23/1961	BOS	L (-13)	48	12	34	0.353	7	12	0.583	30	5		1	31
18	11/25/1961	CHP	W (+32)	48	15	37	0.405	9	12	0.750	38	3		2	39
19	11/28/1961	STL	W (+10)	48	13	28	0.464	13	25	0.520	22	1		0	39
20	12/1/1961	LAL	W (+21)	48	22	47	0.468	16	26	0.615	21	4		1	60
21	12/2/1961	LAL	L (-10)	48	11	22	0.500	15	26	0.577	24	1		1	37

G	Date	Opp	W/L	MP	FG	FGA	FG%	FT	FTA	FT%	TRB	AST	BLK	PF	PTS
22	12/5/1961	NYK	W (+17)	48	17	31	0.548	5	12	0.417	22	4		1	39
23	12/6/1961	STL	L (-5)	48	12	27	0.444	15	20	0.75	16	1		2	39
24	12/8/1961	LAL	L (-4)	63	31	62	0.5	16	31	0.516	43	1		4	78
25	12/9/1961	CHP	W (+22)	48	28	48	0.583	5	10	0.5	36	0		3	61
26	12/10/1961	CHP	W (+9)	48	23	44	0.523	9	16	0.563	16	2		4	55
27	12/12/1961	DET	W (+23)	48	22	42	0.524	10	14	0.714	25	5		2	54
28	12/13/1961	BOS	L (-10)	48	22	43	0.512	8	12	0.667	30	0		2	52
29	12/14/1961	SYR	W (+11)	48	17	39	0.436	9	17	0.529	22	2		1	43
30	12/16/1961	CHP	W (+2)	48	21	39	0.538	8	12	0.667	21	3		3	50
31	12/19/1961	CIN	W (+7)	48	24	47	0.511	9	14	0.643	25	1		0	57
32	12/20/1961	DET	W (+15)	48	24	47	0.511	7	11	0.636	19	6		0	55
33	12/25/1961	NYK	L (-1)	58	23	44	0.523	13	22	0.591	36	0		3	59
34	12/26/1961	SYR	W (+7)	48	21	53	0.396	9	15	0.6	29	1		2	51
35	12/27/1961	NYK	W (+12)	48	20	42	0.476	13	18	0.722	30	4		3	53
36	12/29/1961	LAL	W (+5)	48	24	43	0.558	12	19	0.632	26	3		1	60
37	12/30/1961	BOS	L (-5)	53	17	34	0.5	7	13	0.538	28	3		2	41
38	1/1/1962	LAL	L (-3)	48	13	29	0.448	6	12	0.5	20	3		1	32
39	1/3/1962	LAL	L (-1)	40	14	25	0.56	8	12	0.667	18	2		1	36
40	1/5/1962	STL	W (+18)	48	20	39	0.513	13	21	0.619	22	2		0	53
41	1/7/1962	STL	L (-25)	48	23	41	0.561	9	17	0.529	21	2		3	55
42	1/9/1962	SYR	L (-9)	48	18	37	0.486	11	21	0.524	27	1		3	47

G	Date	Opp	W/L	MP	FG	FGA	FG%	FT	FTA	FT%	TRB	AST	BLK	PF	PTS
43	1/10/1962	DET	W (+3)	48	15	40	0.375	9	13	0.692	25	1		0	39
44	1/11/1962	CIN	L (-17)	48	19	40	0.475	14	24	0.583	22	5		0	52
45	1/13/1962	CHP	W (+18)	48	29	48	0.604	15	25	0.600	36	0		2	73
46	1/14/1962	BOS	L (-9)	48	27	45	0.600	8	11	0.727	28	2		1	62
47	1/17/1962	STL	W (+6)	53	24	48	0.500	14	20	0.700	23	4		3	62
48	1/18/1962	CIN	L (-18)	48	22	50	0.440	10	16	0.625	31	3		3	54
49	1/19/1962	DET	W (+11)	48	23	42	0.548	7	10	0.700	21	2		1	53
50	1/20/1962	DET	W (+16)	48	17	39	0.436	10	14	0.714	28	5		3	44
51	1/21/1962	SYR	W (+7)	53	25	42	0.595	12	17	0.706	23	3		1	62
52	1/24/1962	CHP	W (+14)	48	23	56	0.411	9	11	0.818	32	5		1	55
53	1/26/1962	STL	W (+26)	48	16	29	0.552	15	19	0.789	22	4		3	47
54	1/27/1962	BOS	W (+25)	48	21	28	0.750	11	17	0.647	27	1		3	53
55	1/28/1962	BOS	W (+4)	53	17	31	0.548	16	22	0.727	20	3		4	50
56	1/30/1962	NYK	L (-6)	48	22	40	0.550	11	19	0.579	27	3		1	55
57	2/1/1962	CIN	W (+21)	48	22	36	0.611	9	16	0.563	26	5		1	53
58	2/2/1962	NYK	W (+13)	48	12	31	0.387	11	19	0.579	19	4		1	35
59	2/3/1962	SYR	L (-22)	48	15	35	0.429	11	14	0.786	15	3		0	41
60	2/4/1962	SYR	W (+11)	48	19	35	0.543	12	18	0.667	26	2		0	50
61	2/8/1962	NYK	W (+16)	48	23	37	0.622	13	19	0.684	24	0		0	59
62	2/9/1962	BOS	W (+2)	48	15	32	0.469	18	23	0.783	29	1		1	48
63	2/10/1962	BOS	W (+1)	48	16	33	0.485	6	12	0.500	31	4		1	38

G	Date	Opp	W/L	MP	FG	FGA	FG%	FT	FTA	FT%	TRB	AST	BLK	PF	PTS
64	2/11/1962	NYK	W (+10)	48	18	36	0.500	6	13	0.462	25	5		0	42
65	2/13/1962	CIN	L (-20)	48	24	40	0.600	17	30	0.567	22	4		3	65
66	2/14/1962	DET	L (-9)	48	17	38	0.447	8	13	0.615	27	3		1	42
67	2/16/1962	CIN	W (+4)	48	18	37	0.486	12	17	0.706	23	4		0	48
68	2/17/1962	STL	L (-7)	48	26	44	0.591	15	20	0.75	28	2		1	67
69	2/20/1962	CHP	W (+5)	48	21	46	0.457	6	8	0.75	21	2		4	48
70	2/21/1962	SYR	L (-41)	48	19	33	0.576	8	17	0.471	16	2		3	46
71	2/22/1962	STL	W (+18)	48	21	36	0.583	19	34	0.559	26	1		0	61
72	2/24/1962	BOS	L (-23)	48	11	24	0.458	4	13	0.308	31	0		1	26
73	2/25/1962	NYK	L (-14)	48	25	38	0.658	17	22	0.773	21	1		1	67
74	2/27/1962	STL	W (+10)	48	25	43	0.581	15	20	0.75	23	2		3	65
75	2/28/1962	CHP	W (+9)	48	24	46	0.522	13	17	0.765	28	6		4	61
76	3/2/1962	NYK	W (+22)	48	36	63	0.571	28	32	0.875	25	2		2	100
77	3/4/1962	NYK	W (+1)	48	24	41	0.585	10	16	0.625	35	4		0	58
78	3/7/1962	BOS	L (-51)	48	13	30	0.433	4	11	0.364	27	2		1	30
79	3/11/1962	SYR	L (-18)	48	19	27	0.704	6	18	0.333	26	2		2	44
80	3/14/1962	CHP	W (+4)	53	15	34	0.441	4	5	0.800	33	4	20	3	34

G	Date	Opp	W/L	MP	FG	FGA	FG%	FT	FTA	FT%	TRB	AST	BLK	PF	PTS
1	3/16/1962	SYR	W (+7)	48	11	29	0.379	10	12	0.833	25	5		2	32
2	3/18/1962	SYR	W (+15)	48	12	26	0.462	4	7	0.571	26	4		1	28
3	3/19/1962	SYR	L (-1)	48	18	32	0.563	4	7	0.571	25	4		4	40
4	3/20/1962	SYR	L (-7)	48	11	24	0.458	7	11	0.636	20	3		2	29
5	3/22/1962	SYR	W (+17)	48	22	48	0.458	12	22	0.545	35	1	12	2	56
6	3/24/1962	BOS	L (-28)	48	13	25	0.520	7	12	0.583	31	3		3	33
7	3/27/1962	BOS	W (+7)	48	16	31	0.516	10	17	0.588	37	5		1	42
8	3/28/1962	BOS	L (-15)	48	14	32	0.438	7	12	0.583	29	6		2	35
9	3/31/1962	BOS	W (+4)	48	15	29	0.517	11	22	0.500	34	2		2	41
10	4/1/1962	BOS	L (-15)	48	11	27	0.407	8	9	0.889	14	0		4	30
11	4/3/1962	BOS	W (+10)	48	12	29	0.414	8	10	0.800	21	1		1	32
12	4/5/1962	BOS	L (-2)	48	7	15	0.467	8	9	0.889	22	3		3	22

G	Date	Opp	W/L	MP	FG	FGA	FG%	FT	FTA	FT%	TRB	AST	BLK	PF	PTS
1	10/23/1962	DET	W (+27)	48	23	35	0.657	10	17	0.588	29	4		0	56
2	10/26/1962	DET	W (+1)	53	20	29	0.690	10	19	0.526	41	1		0	50
3	10/27/1962	CHZ	W (+3)	53	18	40	0.450	10	12	0.833	23	3		1	46
4	10/28/1962	CIN	L (-1)	53	23	60	0.383	7	17	0.412	27	2		2	53
5	10/30/1962	NYK	W (+19)	48	24	44	0.545	11	12	0.917	35	6		0	59
6	11/2/1962	NYK	W (+22)	48	16	25	0.640	12	19	0.632	23	4		0	44
7	11/3/1962	LAL	L (-12)	48	29	48	0.604	14	18	0.778	18	1		0	72
8	11/7/1962	LAL	L (-24)	48	16	32	0.500	6	10	0.600	29	4		2	38
9	11/9/1962	CHZ	W (+8)	48	21	31	0.677	12	15	0.800	27	7		3	54
10	11/10/1962	CHZ	W (+5)	48	24	51	0.471	9	12	0.750	28	3		1	57
11	11/13/1962	STL	L (-32)	48	18	34	0.529	9	19	0.474	24	2		3	45
12	11/14/1962	DET	L (-8)	48	18	40	0.450	13	21	0.619	25	1		1	49
13	11/16/1962	NYK	W (+16)	48	29	43	0.674	15	19	0.789	14	1		0	73
14	11/17/1962	BOS	L (-18)	48	16	31	0.516	13	24	0.542	27	2		1	45
15	11/18/1962	CIN	L (-12)	48	24	51	0.471	11	16	0.688	17	0		2	59
16	11/21/1962	CIN	L (-4)	48	27	52	0.519	7	15	0.467	22	3		3	61
17	11/23/1962	LAL	L (-5)	48	20	36	0.556	13	22	0.591	24	3		2	53
18	11/25/1962	CIN	L (-13)	48	15	33	0.455	11	15	0.733	23	3		2	41
19	11/27/1962	CHZ	L (-8)	48	15	32	0.469	7	9	0.778	37	0		3	37
20	11/29/1962	STL	L (-7)	48	20	29	0.690	13	24	0.542	34	4		1	53
21	12/2/1962	STL	L (-6)	48	25	36	0.694	9	14	0.643	24	2		1	59

G	Date	Opp	W/L	MP	FG	FGA	FG%	FT	FTA	FT%	TRB	AST	BLK	PF	PTS
22	12/7/1962	DET	L (-7)	48	21	46	0.457	9	18	0.500	18				51
23	12/8/1962	STL	L (-16)	36	17	30	0.567	5	9	0.556	16	4		1	39
24	12/9/1962	CHZ	L (-8)	48	12	33	0.364	5	14	0.357	21	4		1	29
25	12/11/1962	SYR	W (+12)	48	27	57	0.474	7	11	0.636	26	1		0	61
26	12/14/1962	LAL	L (-2)	48	24	41	0.585	15	20	0.750	30	1		4	63
27	12/15/1962	LAL	L (-9)	48	10	24	0.417	4	8	0.500	15			4	24
28	12/16/1962	SYR	L (-7)	48	18	32	0.563	7	12	0.583	17	2		3	43
29	12/18/1962	STL	W (+20)	45	26	53	0.491	9	14	0.643	20	2		0	61
30	12/21/1962	DET	W (+9)	48	23	42	0.548	6	12	0.500	27			3	52
31	12/22/1962	SYR	W (+5)	48	16	33	0.485	7	14	0.500	28	4		1	39
32	12/25/1962	STL	W (+3)	48	14	23	0.609	4	11	0.364	20	0		0	32
33	12/26/1962	BOS	L (-3)	48	16	36	0.444	11	16	0.688	32	4	12	1	43
34	12/27/1962	BOS	L (-6)	48	14	24	0.583	4	7	0.571	27	1		3	32
35	12/28/1962	SYR	W (+7)	48	17	40	0.425	2	9	0.222	25	3		2	36
36	12/29/1962	NYK	W (+5)	48	14	32	0.438	5	13	0.385	23	3		0	33
37	1/2/1963	BOS	L (-15)	53	8	20	0.400	7	15	0.467	31	3		2	23
38	1/4/1963	CIN	L (-1)	48	19	42	0.452	7	14	0.500	26	0		2	45
39	1/5/1963	CHZ	W (+1)	48	18	44	0.409	14	14	1.000	25	2		4	50
40	1/6/1963	STL	L (-11)	48	17	26	0.654	7	15	0.467	22	1		1	41
41	1/8/1963	BOS	L (-6)	48	18	26	0.692	9	13	0.692	31	0		1	45
42	1/11/1963	LAL	L (-5)	48	28	47	0.596	11	17	0.647	25	1		1	67

G	Date	Opp	W/L	MP	FG	FGA	FG%	FT	FTA	FT%	TRB	AST	BLK	PF	PTS
43	1/12/1963	LAL	L (-5)	48	15	32	0.469	10	17	0.588	24	4		2	40
44	1/14/1963	NYK	W (+8)	48	17	35	0.486	14	23	0.609	33	4		2	48
45	1/17/1963	NYK	L (-13)	48	11	25	0.440	6	12	0.500	27	1		2	28
46	1/19/1963	STL	L (-2)	48	15	25	0.600	5	9	0.556	21	1		2	35
47	1/20/1963	STL	L (-1)	4:00	3	4	0.750	0	1	0.000	1	0		0	6
48	1/22/1963	DET	L (-8)	48	17	34	0.500	5	13	0.385	25	3		3	39
49	1/24/1963	DET	W (+24)	43	25	36	0.694	8	11	0.727	23	4		2	58
50	1/26/1963	SYR	L (-6)	48	16	26	0.615	3	6	0.500	22	4		3	35
51	1/27/1963	SYR	L (-9)	48	15	34	0.441	10	14	0.714	31	2		4	40
52	1/29/1963	NYK	W (+20)	48	27	44	0.614	8	17	0.471	12	0		1	62
53	1/30/1963	BOS	L (-14)	48	20	41	0.488	10	14	0.714	17	0		1	50
54	2/1/1963	CIN	W (+7)	48	17	44	0.386	10	15	0.667	15	4		1	44
55	2/3/1963	CHZ	L (-2)	48	15	27	0.556	4	7	0.571	20	6		1	34
56	2/5/1963	CHZ	W (+2)	48	13	22	0.591	10	19	0.526	22	6		4	36
57	2/6/1963	DET	W (+1)	48	21	42	0.500	6	10	0.600	19	5		0	48
58	2/7/1963	CIN	L (-5)	48	23	46	0.500	10	16	0.625	19	5		1	56
59	2/9/1963	BOS	L (-6)	48	7	19	0.368	17	24	0.708	27	4		1	31
60	2/10/1963	SYR	L (-24)	45	12	21	0.571	5	10	0.500	23	5		1	29
61	2/12/1963	DET	L (-5)	48	20	35	0.571	6	8	0.750	32	7		1	46
62	2/13/1963	DET	L (-2)	53	20	38	0.526	11	19	0.579	29	11		4	51
63	2/16/1963	LAL	W (+4)	58	26	47	0.553	4	11	0.364	21	3		1	56

G	Date	Opp	W/L	MP	FG	FGA	FG%	FT	FTA	FT%	TRB	AST	BLK	PF	PTS
64	2/19/1963	LAL	W (+2)	48	13	33	0.394	13	18	0.722	36	7		1	39
65	2/21/1963	BOS	L (-17)	48	16	29	0.552	8	11	0.727	38	4		3	40
66	2/22/1963	NYK	L (-13)	48	15	29	0.517	7	13	0.538	18	2		1	37
67	2/23/1963	CHZ	W (+4)	48	14	43	0.326	6	9	0.667	22	0		3	34
68	2/24/1963	STL	L (-21)	40	6	11	0.545	1	1	1.000	12	4		2	13
69	2/26/1963	BOS	W (+16)	48	15	27	0.556	4	8	0.500	30	8		1	34
70	3/1/1963	CIN	W (+7)	48	23	44	0.523	8	12	0.667	27	5		4	54
71	3/2/1963	LAL	W (+9)	48	23	35	0.657	3	12	0.250	20	4		1	49
72	3/3/1963	CIN	W (+1)	48	17	37	0.459	11	15	0.733	33	10		1	45
73	3/5/1963	DET	L (-9)	48	10	22	0.455	5	8	0.625	19	10		2	25
74	3/6/1963	CHZ	L (-10)	48	20	31	0.645	11	20	0.550	22	5		4	51
75	3/8/1963	DET	L (-8)	53	23	43	0.535	5	11	0.455	25	5		2	51
76	3/10/1963	SYR	L (-15)	48	27	38	0.711	16	22	0.727	18	3		2	70
77	3/12/1963	LAL	W (+6)	48	18	29	0.621	6	13	0.462	28	9		1	42
78	3/14/1963	STL	L (-5)	48	17	21	0.810	5	8	0.625	28	1		2	39
79	3/15/1963	STL	W (+11)	48	14	20	0.700	10	13	0.769	27	6		1	38
80	3/16/1963	LAL	L (-6)	53	16	38	0.421	8	16	0.500	17	4		2	4

G	Date	Opp	W/L	MP	FG	FGA	FG%	FT	FTA	FT%	TRB	AST	BLK	PF	PTS
1	10/19/1963	BAL	W (+1)	45	10	19	0.526	3	6	0.500	16	3		4	23
2	10/22/1963	CIN	L (-6)	43	13	24	0.542	10	16	0.625	27	3		0	36
3	10/23/1963	STL	W (+4)	44	9	16	0.563	4	7	0.571	18	2		2	22
4	10/26/1963	CIN	W (+3)	46	8	20	0.400	5	6	0.833	20	5		0	21
5	10/29/1963	CIN	L (-7)	39	13	23	0.565	6	13	0.462	18	4		3	32
6	11/2/1963	LAL	W (+19)	48	23	41	0.561	9	15	0.600	29	6		3	55
7	11/7/1963	NYK	W (+22)	37	9	20	0.4500	5	13	0.385	16	4		1	23
8	11/8/1963	LAL	L (-3)	43	13	27	0.481	7	18	0.389	19	5		4	33
9	11/9/1963	NYK	L (-5)	48	14	25	0.560	2	7	0.286	37	4		2	30
10	11/12/1963	PHI	L (-4)	51	13	30	0.433	5	10	0.500	26	4		2	31
11	11/13/1963	CIN	W (+6)	48	20	38	0.526	9	13	0.692	22	3		3	49
12	11/14/1963	STL	L (-12)	45	11	24	0.458	12	17	0.706	22	3		3	34
13	11/15/1963	DET	L (-3)	43	9	22	0.409	5	9	0.556	22	9		2	23
14	11/17/1963	DET	W (+24)	38	17	31	0.548	3	6	0.500	19	5		2	37
15	11/19/1963	STL	W (+33)	42	17	25	0.680	6	13	0.462	25	9		4	40
16	11/26/1963	CIN	L (-11)	42	8	20	0.400	7	12	0.583	19	4		2	23
17	11/27/1963	NYK	W (+29)	33	18	19	0.947	2	3	0.667	17	4		3	38
18	11/29/1963	BAL	L (-1)	44	14	31	0.452	10	14	0.714	13	3		1	38
19	11/30/1963	BOS	L (-13)	46	10	18	0.556	3	9	0.333	22	6		1	23
20	12/3/1963	NYK	W (+8)	41	7	15	0.467	7	11	0.636	22	6	10	1	21
21	12/4/1963	STL	L (-22)	40	9	21	0.429	3	8	0.375	17	3		1	21

G	Date	Opp	W/L	MP	FG	FGA	FG%	FT	FTA	FT%	TRB	AST	BLK	PF	PTS
22	12/6/1963	LAL	L (-7)	48	22	45	0.489	15	29	0.517	27	4		1	59
23	12/8/1963	LAL	W (+2)	42	13	27	0.481	5	14	0.357	20	3		3	31
24	12/10/1963	BAL	W (+9)	47	21	36	0.583	7	9	0.778	21	4		4	49
25	12/13/1963	BAL	L (-2)	53	18	36	0.500	7	13	0.538	26	4		4	43
26	12/15/1963	BAL	W (+25)	43	20	36	0.556	4	7	0.571	34	4		1	44
27	12/17/1963	STL	W (+4)	44	15	24	0.625	4	8	0.500	30	4		3	34
28	12/18/1963	STL	W (+8)		9			9	16	0.563	27	11		2	27
29	12/20/1963	PHI	L (-2)	48	16	26	0.615	9	18	0.500	27	8		3	41
30	12/22/1963	PHI	W (+14)	47	18	27	0.667	4	9	0.444	23	12		0	40
31	12/26/1963	PHI	L (-6)	48	16	31	0.516	17	22	0.773	13	5		3	49
32	12/28/1963	BAL	W (+2)	48	11	24	0.458	4	8	0.500	19	6		3	26
33	12/30/1963	DET	L (-2)	53	16	35	0.457	15	24	0.625	26	6		1	47
34	12/31/1963	NYK	W (+22)	46	16	33	0.485	10	18	0.556	27	7		3	42
35	1/2/1964	STL	L (-5)	48	18	31	0.581	6	11	0.545	21	4		4	42
36	1/3/1964	BOS	L (-10)	48	10	18	0.556	4	13	0.308	24	5		4	24
37	1/7/1964	BOS	W (+3)	46	15	28	0.536	5	14	0.357	32	1		1	35
38	1/9/1964	NYK	W (+15)		16	32	0.500	11	16	0.688	26			0	43
39	1/10/1964	LAL	W (+25)	47	22	36	0.611	6	13	0.462	23	6		1	50
40	1/12/1964	NYK	W (+7)	48	20	35	0.571	7	9	0.778	23	4		1	47
41	1/15/1964	DET	W (+10)	48	12	24	0.500	8	17	0.471	18	3		3	32
42	1/17/1964	PHI	W (+21)	47	14	32	0.438	8	10	0.800	29	8		2	36

G	Date	Opp	W/L	MP	FG	FGA	FG%	FT	FTA	FT%	TRB	AST	BLK	PF	PTS
43	1/18/1964	BAL	L (-7)	47	14	30	0.467	0	1	0.000	23	3		4	28
44	1/19/1964	BOS	L (-3)	48	14	31	0.452	3	6	0.500	30	3		4	31
45	1/21/1964	DET	W (+12)	46	11	28	0.393	2	8	0.250	19	2		1	24
46	1/23/1964	DET	W (+32)	36	12	20	0.600	4	13	0.308	15	5		1	28
47	1/24/1964	LAL	L (-18)	45	16	33	0.485	9	21	0.429	18	4		2	41
48	1/25/1964	LAL	W (+25)	44	16	30	0.533	8	17	0.471	18	5		0	40
49	1/26/1964	LAL	L (-12)	48	18	49	0.367	13	24	0.542	19	2		4	49
50	1/28/1964	PHI	W (+22)	47	24	36	0.667	11	20	0.550	13	9		2	59
51	1/29/1964	BOS	W (+8)	48	11	25	0.440	6	11	0.545	22	4		1	28
52	1/30/1964	DET	L (-9)	48	15	30	0.500	12	18	0.667	19	6		3	42
53	2/1/1964	NYK	W (+19)	44	18	28	0.643	4	8	0.500	16	6		5	40
54	2/2/1964	BAL	W (+2)	53	13	33	0.394	6	7	0.857	16	4		3	32
55	2/4/1964	DET	W (+39)	44	16	26	0.615	6	12	0.500	21	9		0	38
56	2/6/1964	DET	W (+7)	48	16	37	0.432	8	12	0.667	23	8		2	40
57	2/8/1964	STL	W (+6)	48	10	21	0.476	10	16	0.625	17	2		4	30
58	2/9/1964	STL	L (-5)	48	14	20	0.700	4	9	0.444	20	2		1	32
59	2/11/1964	DET	W (+10)	53	25	50	0.500	9	21	0.429	18	4		4	59
60	2/13/1964	BOS	W (+11)	48	12	20	0.600	6	13	0.462	24	5		1	30
61	2/15/1964	BOS	L (-9)	48	13	20	0.650	6	13	0.462	33	3		5	32
62	2/17/1964	CIN	L (-16)	48	22	41	0.537	8	12	0.667	23	5		4	52
63	2/18/1964	DET	W (+10)	48	20	37	0.541	12	16	0.750	32	2		3	52

G	Date	Opp	W/L	MP	FG	FGA	FG%	FT	FTA	FT%	TRB	AST	BLK	PF	PTS
64	2/19/1964	CIN	W (+7)		14			4	12	0.333	19			1	32
65	2/21/1964	CIN	L (-8)	48	18	30	0.600	4	14	0.286	27	3		2	40
66	2/23/1964	LAL	W (+1)	48	16	40	0.400	5	11	0.455	25	6		3	37
67	2/25/1964	CIN	W (+9)	47	22	40	0.550	8	16	0.500	22	4		3	52
68	2/27/1964	STL	W (+10)	48	18	29	0.621	4	11	0.364	31	2		2	40
69	2/28/1964	BOS	L (-15)	48	12	23	0.522	6	13	0.462	28	2		3	30
70	2/29/1964	NYK	W (+26)	46	16	31	0.516	5	10	0.500	28	7		3	37
71	3/1/1964	DET	W (+14)	48	15	37	0.405	8	16	0.500	20	2		0	38
72	3/2/1964	STL	L (-9)	48	9	19	0.474	9	16	0.563	23	4		3	27
73	3/5/1964	STL	L (-2)	48	15	25	0.600	14	25	0.560	23	2		2	44
74	3/7/1964	LAL	W (+2)	48	21	46	0.457	5	14	0.357	13	10		4	47
75	3/10/1964	BAL	W (+18)	46	16	21	0.762	0	3	0.000	22	13		2	32
76	3/12/1964	BAL	W (+23)	42	17	23	0.739	1	5	0.200	21	5		2	35
77	3/13/1964	LAL	L (-3)	48	14	29	0.483	7	11	0.636	24	8		2	35
78	3/14/1964	LAL	W (+16)	47	22	38	0.579	11	18	0.611	14	8		0	55
79	3/16/1964	PHI	L (-1)		12			6	11	0.545	15	14		2	30
80	3/18/1964	PHI	W (+4)	48	14	24	0.583	8	10	0.800	33	8		3	36

G	Date	Opp	W/L	MP	FG	FGA	FG%	FT	FTA	FT%	TRB	AST	BLK	PF	PTS
1	4/1/1964	STL	L (-5)	48	15	28	0.536	7	9	0.778	22	2		3	37
2	4/3/1964	STL	W (+35)	45	11	23	0.478	6	15	0.400	27	5		3	28
3	4/5/1964	STL	L (-4)	48	19	36	0.528	8	16	0.500	23	2		5	46
4	4/8/1964	STL	W (+2)	48	14	30	0.467	8	15	0.533	23	3		0	36
5	4/10/1964	STL	W (+24)	45	22	32	0.688	6	10	0.600	15	6		1	50
6	4/12/1964	STL	L (-28)	46	13	24	0.542	8	15	0.533	24	3		1	34
7	4/16/1964	STL	W (+10)	48	19	29	0.655	1	6	0.167	30	6	12	2	39
8	4/18/1964	BOS	L (-12)	44	9	20	0.450	4	12	0.333	23	1		4	22
9	4/20/1964	BOS	L (-23)	44	14	27	0.519	4	9	0.444	25	3		2	32
10	4/22/1964	BOS	W (+24)	45	15	22	0.682	5	11	0.455	25	5		0	35
11	4/24/1964	BOS	L (-3)	48	12	23	0.522	3	8	0.375	38	1		1	27
12	4/26/1964	BOS	L (-6)	48	12	28	0.429	6	13	0.462	27	2		5	30

G	Date	Opp	W/L	MP	FG	FGA	FG%	FT	FTA	FT%	TRB	AST	BLK	PF	PTS
1	10/31/1964	BAL	L (-4)	38	8	18	0.444	0	1	0.000	17	2		2	16
2	11/4/1964	STL	L (-1)	48	17	26	0.654	3	13	0.231	27	2		3	37
3	11/6/1964	NYK	W (+6)	58	21	43	0.488	10	22	0.455	21	3		1	52
4	11/7/1964	LAL	L (-27)	39	8	23	0.348	5	9	0.556	21	5		2	21
5	11/8/1964	NYK	W (+9)	43	17	33	0.515	7	16	0.438	21	4		4	41
6	11/10/1964	PHI	W (+11)	46	16	39	0.410	4	10	0.400	18	1		3	36
7	11/11/1964	BOS	L (-26)	43	10	24	0.417	4	9	0.444	22	1		1	24
8	11/12/1964	DET	L (-22)	48	22	46	0.478	9	22	0.409	23	2		3	53
9	11/14/1964	STL	L (-14)	45	8	23	0.348	7	17	0.412	22	4		2	23
10	11/15/1964	CIN	W (+16)	48	26	44	0.591	10	21	0.476	22	1		1	62
11	11/17/1964	CIN	L (-6)	48	18	38	0.474	9	20	0.450	24	1		2	45
12	11/21/1964	CIN	L (-7)	48	20	35	0.571	6	12	0.500	21	3		1	46
13	11/22/1964	DET	L (-2)	48	21	39	0.538	8	21	0.381	40	0		1	50
14	11/24/1964	NYK	L (-8)	48	16	29	0.552	4	12	0.333	22	6		3	36
15	11/25/1964	BOS	L (-4)	48	17	44	0.386	3	9	0.333	32	5		3	37
16	11/26/1964	PHI	L (-11)	48	27	58	0.466	9	20	0.450	32	3		2	63
17	11/28/1964	LAL	W (+3)	48	17	33	0.515	6	21	0.286	30	6		2	40
18	12/1/1964	BAL	W (+1)	58	22	48	0.458	12	20	0.600	29	3		4	56
19	12/2/1964	BAL	L (-6)	48	14	28	0.500	5	11	0.455	28	4		4	33
20	12/4/1964	BOS	W (+27)	30	11	19	0.579	2	10	0.200	27	3		1	24
21	12/5/1964	BOS	L (-24)	32	4	12	0.333	0	1	0.000	18	2		0	8

G	Date	Opp	W/L	MP	FG	FGA	FG%	FT	FTA	FT%	TRB	AST	BLK	PF	PTS
22	12/11/1964	DET	L (-4)	45	17	32	0.531	6	15	0.400	17	3		1	40
23	12/12/1964	DET	W (+17)	44	15	26	0.577	3	11	0.273	17	3		1	33
24	12/14/1964	PHI	L (-7)	48	17	34	0.500	6	15	0.400	24	3		3	40
25	12/15/1964	NYK	W (+2)	53	25	45	0.556	8	19	0.421	22	5		2	58
26	12/16/1964	BOS	L (-1)	48	13	30	0.433	5	10	0.500	24	2		3	31
27	12/18/1964	PHI	W (+6)	45	19	31	0.613	3	10	0.300	24	5		2	41
28	12/20/1964	PHI	L (-2)	48	18	35	0.514	9	12	0.750	21	2		1	45
29	12/22/1964	NYK	L (-6)	45	19	39	0.487	8	12	0.667	18	4		2	46
30	12/26/1964	LAL	L (-7)	46	18	36	0.500	5	14	0.357	22	4		4	41
31	12/28/1964	CIN	L (-5)	46	19	35	0.543	4	14	0.286	20	2		1	42
32	12/29/1964	STL	L (-18)	39	14	25	0.560	7	13	0.538	16	1		3	35
33	12/30/1964	NYK	L (-16)	45	17	35	0.486	7	17	0.412	32	5		1	41
34	1/1/1965	NYK	L (-1)	48	14	35	0.400	1	8	0.125	17	6		1	29
35	1/2/1965	BAL	L (-26)	41	20	42	0.476	3	7	0.429	23	2		3	43
36	1/3/1965	BAL	L (-10)	43	24	42	0.571	5	8	0.625	28	4		0	53
37	1/6/1965	PHI	L (-19)	48	13	29	0.448	3	8	0.375	26	4		1	29
38	1/8/1965	BOS	L (-3)	46	14	22	0.636	2	8	0.250	25	1		2	30
39	1/21/1965	SFW	W (+9)	44	9	17	0.529	4	10	0.400	29	1	11	4	22
40	1/22/1965	DET	W (+6)		10	26	0.385	1	10	0.100	32	4		1	21
41	1/23/1965	BOS	W (+4)		7	20	0.350	2	5	0.400	26	6		3	16
42	1/26/1965	DET	L (-2)		7	22	0.318	3	5	0.600	22	5		1	17

G	Date	Opp	W/L	MP	FG	FGA	FG%	FT	FTA	FT%	TRB	AST	BLK	PF	PTS
43	1/27/1965	BOS	L (-17)	40	13	21	0.619	2	6	0.333	19	5		4	28
44	1/29/1965	BOS	W (+13)	40	11	21	0.524	5	9	0.556	34	9		1	27
45	1/31/1965	CIN	W (+5)		15			6	12	0.500	17	3			36
46	2/2/1965	STL	W (+14)	45	8	18	0.444	8	13	0.615	16	5		2	24
47	2/3/1965	NYK	W (+21)		14	25	0.560	1	6	0.167	13	0		2	29
48	2/4/1965	STL	W (+4)		14	30	0.467	7	11	0.636	31	3		1	35
49	2/6/1965	CIN	W (+5)		13	25	0.520	5	8	0.625	14	4		5	31
50	2/8/1965	LAL	L (-19)		5	15	0.333	6	10	0.600	17	4		1	16
51	2/9/1965	SFW	W (+18)	42	13	25	0.520	7	14	0.500	18	4	16	3	33
52	2/10/1965	LAL	W (+11)		14	26	0.538	3	11	0.273	21	4		2	31
53	2/11/1965	SFW	L (-6)	47	7	21	0.333	10	19	0.526	27	2		0	24
54	2/13/1965	CIN	L (-2)		13	22	0.591	11	16	0.688	30	2		4	37
55	2/18/1965	LAL	L (-7)		17	29	0.586	6	12	0.500	18	4		3	40
56	2/20/1965	NYK	W (+19)	46	14	22	0.636	9	12	0.750	32	2		3	37
57	2/21/1965	BAL	W (+1)		16	26	0.615	8	11	0.727	18	2		1	40
58	2/22/1965	BAL	W (+10)		14	25	0.560	7	12	0.583	18	4		3	35
59	2/23/1965	NYK	L (-28)	40	9	15	0.600	12	19	0.632	18	1		1	30
60	2/24/1965	DET	L (-2)		14	27	0.519	4	5	0.800	21	4		1	32
61	2/28/1965	LAL	L (-4)		14	24	0.583	6	14	0.429	30	2		1	34
62	3/2/1965	LAL	L (-9)		7	20	0.350	2	4	0.500	20	4		1	16
63	3/3/1965	STL	L (-14)	45	13	24	0.542	5	10	0.500	18	2		0	31

G	Date	Opp	W/L	MP	FG	FGA	FG%	FT	FTA	FT%	TRB	AST	BLK	PF	PTS
64	3/5/1965	CIN	W (+1)		17	32	0.531	14	25	0.56	22	1		1	48
65	3/6/1965	BOS	W (+5)		10	22	0.455	7	17	0.412	43	8		4	27
66	3/7/1965	BOS	L (-22)	41	12	23	0.522	3	5	0.6	22	4		3	27
67	3/9/1965	NYK	L (-2)	53	18	30	0.6	1	11	0.091	28	3		1	37
68	3/10/1965	NYK	L (-11)	44	12	25	0.48	3	7	0.429	11	6		2	27
69	3/13/1965	DET	W (+15)		12	16	0.75	7	14	0.5	21	6		3	31
70	3/14/1965	BAL	L (-17)		23	35	0.657	5	9	0.556	20	2		2	51
71	3/16/1965	SFW	L (-8)	48	13	20	0.65	8	14	0.571	26	5		0	34
72	3/20/1965	CIN	L (-3)		11	23	0.478	10	12	0.833	14	6		2	32
73	3/21/1965	BAL	W (+22)	41	8	12	0.667	2	3	0.667	14	6		2	18

1965 Playoffs

G	Date	Opp	W/L	MP	FG	FGA	FG%	FT	FTA	FT%	TRB	AST	BLK	PF	PTS
1	3/24/1965	CIN	W (+2)		10	21	0.476	6	18	0.333	23	4		2	26
2	3/26/1965	CIN	L (-1)		12	24	0.500	6	9	0.667	15	10		3	30
3	3/28/1965	CIN	W (+14)	46	6	19	0.316	5	8	0.625	15	6	9	1	17
4	3/31/1965	CIN	W (+7)	48	14	22	0.636	10	16	0.625	26	5	10	3	38
5	4/4/1965	BOS	L (-10)	48	13	22	0.591	7	12	0.583	31	3	11	2	33
6	4/6/1965	BOS	W (+6)	48	12	19	0.632	6	9	0.667	39	8	8	3	30
7	4/8/1965	BOS	L (-18)	48	7	21	0.333	10	15	0.667	37	1		3	24
8	4/9/1965	BOS	W (+3)	53	11	24	0.458	12	20	0.600	34	3		4	34
9	4/11/1965	BOS	L (-6)	48	13	23	0.565	4	8	0.500	21	2	2	2	30
10	4/13/1965	BOS	W (+6)	48	13	22	0.591	4	8	0.500	26	4	2+	5	30
11	4/15/1965	BOS	L (-1)	48	12	15	0.800	6	13	0.462	32	2	1	1	30

G	Date	Opp	W/L	MP	FG	FGA	FG%	FT	FTA	FT%	TRB	AST	BLK	PF	PTS
1	10/16/1965	BAL	W (+32)	40	16	29	0.552	1	8	0.125	25	0		0	33
2	10/23/1965	DET	W (+17)	45	21	25	0.840	11	15	0.733	21	2	15	1	53
3	10/30/1965	CIN	W (+20)	46	18	30	0.600	3	6	0.500	28	10		2	39
4	11/3/1965	DET	L (-10)	48	12	23	0.522	8	15	0.533	27	4		2	32
5	11/4/1965	SFW	L (-2)	48	5	13	0.385	5	10	0.500	21	3		2	15
6	11/5/1965	SFW	W (+18)	43	7	18	0.389	8	15	0.533	21	4		1	22
7	11/6/1965	BOS	L (-10)	48	11	30	0.367	8	14	0.571	24	1		4	30
8	11/9/1965	LAL	W (+8)	48	13	25	0.520	13	17	0.765	24	8		2	39
9	11/11/1965	SFW	W (+8)	48	8	22	0.364	10	13	0.769	28	2		0	26
10	11/12/1965	BOS	W (+9)	48	10	26	0.385	7	8	0.875	32	7		3	27
11	11/13/1965	NYK	W (+8)	46	15	21	0.714	4	8	0.500	17	3		4	34
12	11/16/1965	STL	W (+9)	48	12	20	0.600	6	15	0.400	17	5		5	30
13	11/17/1965	CIN	L (-16)	45	18	29	0.621	10	12	0.833	24	2		1	46
14	11/19/1965	BAL	L (-10)	48	15	34	0.441	6	13	0.462	25	5		5	36
15	11/20/1965	BAL	L (-5)	48	8	20	0.400	5	7	0.714	22	3		2	21
16	11/21/1965	LAL	W (+6)	48	12	31	0.387	8	14	0.571	33	2		3	32
17	11/24/1965	LAL	L (-3)	48	15	26	0.577	12	21	0.571	27	8		3	42
18	11/26/1965	SFW	W (+12)	48	8	22	0.364	9	18	0.500	21	9		2	25
19	11/27/1965	SFW	W (+7)	48	15	32	0.469	8	13	0.615	31	4		1	38
20	11/30/1965	BAL	L (-21)	45	18	34	0.529	5	16	0.313	33	5		3	41
21	12/3/1965	BOS	W (+16)	48	12	19	0.632	4	7	0.571	30	2		3	28

G	Date	Opp	W/L	MP	FG	FGA	FG%	FT	FTA	FT%	TRB	AST	BLK	PF	PTS
22	12/6/1965	LAL	W (+9)	48	13	29	0.448	3	8	0.375	25	3		1	29
23	12/8/1965	BAL	L (-2)	48	19	40	0.475	8	12	0.667	21	0		3	46
24	12/10/1965	DET	L (-2)	48	17	28	0.607	6	10	0.600	29	5		3	40
25	12/11/1965	CIN	W (+3)	53	15	23	0.652	8	14	0.571	33	6		3	38
26	12/14/1965	CIN	L (-3)	48	14	25	0.560	4	11	0.364	20	7		1	32
27	12/15/1965	LAL	W (+14)	48	12	23	0.522	7	8	0.875	23	13		2	31
28	12/17/1965	LAL	W (+10)	48	17	35	0.486	4	7	0.571	24	9		3	38
29	12/18/1965	SFW	W (+4)	53	8	17	0.471	7	14	0.500	27	3		1	23
30	12/20/1965	SFW	L (-6)	48	17	32	0.531	11	22	0.500	21	2		2	45
31	12/26/1965	SFW	W (+14)	47	13	22	0.591	7	11	0.636	30	8	16	4	33
32	12/28/1965	BOS	W (+9)	48	11	25	0.440	9	12	0.750	40	6		2	31
33	12/29/1965	DET	W (+1)	48	14	28	0.500	6	13	0.462	23	3		1	34
34	12/30/1965	STL	L (-17)	44	9	17	0.529	5	12	0.417	14	4		4	23
35	1/2/1966	NYK	W (+11)	47	22	38	0.579	6	11	0.545	23	6		3	50
36	1/4/1966	NYK	W (+2)	48	12	26	0.462	3	15	0.200	20	3		4	27
37	1/6/1966	BAL	W (+6)	47	18	34	0.529	5	8	0.625	28	6		2	41
38	1/7/1966	LAL	L (-6)	48	17	34	0.500	15	22	0.682	30	5		0	49
39	1/8/1966	STL	L (-10)	48	12	27	0.444	5	7	0.714	22	3		2	29
40	1/9/1966	STL	W (+10)	48	16	28	0.571	9	15	0.600	10	3		1	41
41	1/12/1966	DET	L (-18)	44	16	32	0.500	9	18	0.500	28	2		1	41
42	1/14/1966	BOS	W (+12)	48	15	28	0.536	7	14	0.500	42	6		2	37

G	Date	Opp	W/L	MP	FG	FGA	FG%	FT	FTA	FT%	TRB	AST	BLK	PF	PTS
43	1/18/1966	BAL	W (+11)	48	20	32	0.625	4	11	0.364	23	8		3	44
44	1/19/1966	DET	W (+17)	46	13	23	0.565	7	10	0.700	20	6		1	33
45	1/21/1966	NYK	W (+11)	48	10	22	0.455	7	12	0.583	12	4		3	27
46	1/23/1966	STL	W (+6)	48	15	24	0.625	6	14	0.429	27	1		2	36
47	1/24/1966	STL	W (+3)	48	9	19	0.474	4	9	0.444	19	4		4	22
48	1/25/1966	LAL	W (+4)	48	21	41	0.512	11	13	0.846	31	3		0	53
49	1/28/1966	CIN	W (+22)	44	19	28	0.679	5	9	0.556	24	3	6	3	43
50	1/30/1966	DET	W (+19)	45	16	26	0.615	6	11	0.545	23	7	6	1	38
51	2/2/1966	STL	L (-7)	48	9	17	0.529	3	8	0.375	22			2	21
52	2/5/1966	NYK	L (-7)	48	14	23	0.609	6	11	0.545	17	3		3	34
53	2/6/1966	BOS	L (-1)	48	6	12	0.500	2	10	0.200	16	2		2	14
54	2/7/1966	LAL	W (+7)	47	28	43	0.651	9	20	0.450	29	2		3	65
55	2/8/1966	NYK	L (-13)	42	18	27	0.667	2	8	0.250	13	1		2	38
56	2/9/1966	DET	W (+17)	45	14	21	0.667	2	4	0.500	22	8		1	30
57	2/11/1966	CIN	W (+19)	48	12	21	0.571	8	16	0.500	22	7		3	32
58	2/12/1966	BOS	L (-2)	48	11	21	0.524	7	12	0.583	26	4		2	29
59	2/14/1966	DET	W (+26)	47	16	18	0.889	9	17	0.529	23	13		2	41
60	2/15/1966	STL	W (+12)	46	15	24	0.625	4	14	0.286	20	5		5	34
61	2/17/1966	LAL	W (+15)	46	12	12	1.000	6	12	0.500	15	13		0	30
62	2/19/1966	SFW	W (+4)	48	12	22	0.545	6	14	0.429	29	5		0	30
63	2/21/1966	CIN	L (-6)	48	11	20	0.550	2	4	0.500	21	5		1	24

G	Date	Opp	W/L	MP	FG	FGA	FG%	FT	FTA	FT%	TRB	AST	BLK	PF	PTS
64	2/22/1966	DET	W (+5)	48	13	20	0.650	6	12	0.500	19	10		2	32
65	2/23/1966	BAL	L (-4)	48	4	11	0.364	12	23	0.522	31	10		3	20
66	2/25/1966	NYK	W (+6)	48	14	34	0.412	7	7	1.000	26	7		4	35
67	2/26/1966	BAL	W (+16)	46	7	18	0.389	2	8	0.250	23	6		2	16
68	3/1/1966	CIN	L (-2)	48	10	25	0.400	2	9	0.222	24	4		3	22
69	3/3/1966	SFW	W (+10)	48	26	39	0.667	10	19	0.526	37	3		2	62
70	3/4/1966	CIN	W (+4)	48	16	34	0.471	4	14	0.286	20	5		1	36
71	3/5/1966	BOS	W (+17)	45	11	25	0.440	5	11	0.455	36	4		2	27
72	3/6/1966	BOS	W (+3)	48	10	19	0.526	12	25	0.480	30	5		2	32
73	3/8/1966	STL	W (+6)	48	11	20	0.550	1	13	0.077	24	7		3	23
74	3/9/1966	STL	W (+8)	48	13	25	0.520	5	13	0.385	36	5		3	31
75	3/12/1966	NYK	W (+8)	47	10	19	0.526	3	7	0.429	23	12		1	23
76	3/13/1966	NYK	W (+2)	48	10	17	0.588	5	8	0.625	19	10		4	25
77	3/17/1966	NYK	W (+9)	48	16	22	0.727	5	9	0.556	23	6		1	37
78	3/19/1966	CIN	W (+6)	48	16	26	0.615	7	13	0.538	28	12		3	39
79	3/20/1966	BAL	W (+4)	48	10	15	0.667	4	8	0.500	26	3		2	24

G	Date	Opp	W/L	MP	FG	FGA	FG%	FT	FTA	FT%	TRB	AST	BLK	PF	PTS
1	4/3/1966	BOS	L (-19)	48	9	19	0.474	7	15	0.467	32	5		1	25
2	4/6/1966	BOS	L (-21)		9	21	0.429	5	7	0.714	25	2		1	23
3	4/7/1966	BOS	W (+6)	48	12	22	0.545	7	17	0.412	27	4		2	31
4	4/10/1966	BOS	L (-6)	53	7	14	0.500	1	4	0.250	33	3		1	15
5	4/12/1966	BOS	L (-8)	48	19	34	0.559	8	25	0.320	34	1		5	46

G	Date	Opp	W/L	MP	FG	FGA	FG%	FT	FTA	FT%	TRB	AST	BLK	PF	PTS
1	10/15/1966	NYK	W (+16)	39	12	14	0.857	4	9	0.444	21	6		1	28
2	10/21/1966	STL	W (+9)	46	8	19	0.421	7	18	0.389	26	3		2	23
3	10/22/1966	BAL	W (+29)		8	18	0.444	4	8	0.500	19	6			20
4	10/25/1966	BAL	W (+20)		9	15	0.600	2	4	0.500	22	5		2	20
5	10/29/1966	BOS	W (+42)		4	7	0.571	5	10	0.500	31	9		0	13
6	11/3/1966	STL	W (+12)		6	13	0.462	2	9	0.222	24	4		2	14
7	11/4/1966	SFW	W (+5)	48	13	18	0.722	4	12	0.333	26	13		0	30
8	11/5/1966	BOS	L (-18)		8	16	0.500	10	21	0.476	23	3		2	26
9	11/8/1966	DET	W (+18)		8	13	0.615	2	7	0.286	24	4	17	1	18
10	11/11/1966	CHI	W (+13)		18	23	0.783	1	10	0.100	33	7		0	37
11	11/12/1966	CIN	W (+14)		11	17	0.647	4	14	0.286	20	9		3	26
12	11/13/1966	CHI	W (+6)		9	10	0.900	6	17	0.353	22	3		1	24
13	11/15/1966	NYK	W (+4)	48	10	15	0.667	4	13	0.308	28	7		3	24
14	11/16/1966	NYK	W (+9)	48	10	12	0.833	8	16	0.500	30	8		4	28
15	11/18/1966	CHI	W (+25)		9	11	0.818	6	9	0.667	18	8		2	24
16	11/19/1966	CIN	W (+24)		9	14	0.643	2	6	0.333	17	11		1	20
17	11/23/1966	CIN	L (-5)		10	16	0.625	8	16	0.500	22	6		1	28
18	11/24/1966	SFW	W (+17)	46	10	16	0.625	7	14	0.500	31	7		0	27
19	11/25/1966	BAL	W (+14)	43	16	17	0.941	9	11	0.818	19	4		1	41
20	11/26/1966	DET	W (+8)		8	14	0.571	10	16	0.625	24	15		2	26
21	11/29/1966	STL	W (+21)		10	11	0.909	5	7	0.714	27	7		2	25

G	Date	Opp	W/L	MP	FG	FGA	FG%	FT	FTA	FT%	TRB	AST	BLK	PF	PTS
22	11/30/1966	DET	W (+9)		10	12	0.833	3	6	0.500	13	10		2	23
23	12/2/1966	LAL	W (+8)	46	13	13	1.000	2	7	0.286	30	7		2	28
24	12/3/1966	BAL	W (+17)		10	11	0.909	12	15	0.800	17	7		2	32
25	12/6/1966	CHI	W (+10)		11	14	0.786	9	21	0.429	21	4		0	31
26	12/7/1966	CHI	W (+14)		9	11	0.818	3	11	0.273	29	6		1	21
27	12/9/1966	NYK	W (+5)	48	9	13	0.692	2	9	0.222	24	7	6+	4	20
28	12/10/1966	STL	W (+10)	44	5	7	0.714	12	22	0.545	21	6		3	22
29	12/11/1966	BOS	L (-14)	48	5	13	0.385	5	10	0.500	24	6		1	15
30	12/13/1966	NYK	W (+15)	46	8	14	0.571	6	10	0.600	28	6		2	22
31	12/16/1966	STL	W (+11)		9	11	0.818	4	9	0.444	22	10		2	22
32	12/17/1966	DET	W (+15)		11	14	0.786	6	12	0.500	27	12		2	28
33	12/21/1966	LAL	W (+6)		7	8	0.875	5	12	0.417	25	11		3	19
34	12/22/1966	SFW	W (+2)	45	6	12	0.500	2	5	0.400	22	8		2	14
35	12/23/1966	LAL	W (+11)		11	16	0.688	2	5	0.400	26	14		0	24
36	12/26/1966	CIN	W (+16)		16	21	0.762	6	15	0.400	32	10		3	38
37	12/28/1966	BOS	W (+5)		9	15	0.600	6	11	0.545	32	9		1	24
38	12/30/1966	DET	W (+24)	40	8	13	0.615	7	13	0.538	23	7		1	23
39	1/3/1967	NYK	W (+6)	51	15	18	0.833	5	17	0.294	33	4		4	35
40	1/4/1967	CHI	W (+21)		8	10	0.800	5	24	0.208	25	9		0	21
41	1/5/1967	NYK	L (-8)	44	5	11	0.455	3	7	0.429	22	6		3	13
42	1/6/1967	BAL	W (+6)		7	16	0.438	3	14	0.214	29	9		2	17

G	Date	Opp	W/L	MP	FG	FGA	FG%	FT	FTA	FT%	TRB	AST	BLK	PF	PTS
43	1/8/1967	CHI	W (+9)	44	10	15	0.667	5	6	0.833	19	4		2	25
44	1/13/1967	STL	W (+18)	43	9	13	0.692	2	7	0.286	20	8		2	20
45	1/15/1967	BOS	W (+15)	48	7	8	0.875	5	8	0.625	25	5	13	2	19
46	1/17/1967	NYK	W (+8)		8	12	0.667	3	8	0.375	28	7		2	19
47	1/18/1967	DET	W (+8)		5	12	0.417	6	10	0.600	17	8		0	16
48	1/19/1967	CHI	W (+25)		11	11	1.000	5	7	0.714	22	7		1	27
49	1/20/1967	LAL	W (+11)		15	15	1.000	2	6	0.333	30	9		1	32
50	1/23/1967	STL	W (+7)		9	12	0.750	4	7	0.571	27	6		1	22
51	1/24/1967	BOS	L (-12)		7	12	0.583	4	10	0.400	28	10		3	18
52	1/27/1967	CIN	W (+3)		7	12	0.583	3	12	0.250	16	10		2	17
53	1/29/1967	STL	L (-6)		13	20	0.650	3	10	0.300	20	4		3	29
54	2/1/1967	LAL	L (-10)		16	23	0.696	7	18	0.389	28	6		0	39
55	2/2/1967	SFW	L (-17)	31	7	17	0.412	2	10	0.200	26	6	5	3	16
56	2/4/1967	SFW	W (+13)	24	10	11	0.909	3	5	0.600	19	8		3	23
57	2/5/1967	LAL	W (+7)		5	9	0.556	6	9	0.667	22	12		1	16
58	2/7/1967	SFW	W (+3)	48	4	5	0.800	7	11	0.636	26	9		2	15
59	2/8/1967	CIN	W (+12)		10	17	0.588	7	9	0.778	24	13		3	27
60	2/10/1967	LAL	W (+17)		16	21	0.762	5	11	0.455	24	12		0	37
61	2/11/1967	BAL	L (-6)		20	28	0.714	3	11	0.273	23	5			43
62	2/12/1967	BOS	L (-1)		10	19	0.526	8	24	0.333	28	6		1	28
63	2/13/1967	CIN	W (+8)	47	26	34	0.765	6	14	0.429	25	6		3	58

G	Date	Opp	W/L	MP	FG	FGA	FG%	FT	FTA	FT%	TRB	AST	BLK	PF	PTS
64	2/15/1967	DET	W (+6)		8	14	0.571	2	6	0.333	28	10		1	18
65	2/17/1967	CIN	W (+9)		5	6	0.833	5	7	0.714	22	17		3	15
66	2/19/1967	STL	W (+1)		11	11	1.000	0	9	0.000	26	5		1	22
67	2/24/1967	BAL	W (+31)		18	18	1.000	6	14	0.429	30	10		3	42
68	2/28/1967	CIN	W (+20)	33	11	14	0.786	6	13	0.462	36	9		1	28
69	3/1/1967	CHI	L (-7)	45	9	13	0.692	2	12	0.167	13	3		1	20
70	3/2/1967	SFW	W (+8)	48	8	20	0.400	8	17	0.471	38	13		2	24
71	3/3/1967	DET	W (+26)		7	10	0.700	5	9	0.556	21	12		1	19
72	3/5/1967	DET	W (+25)		4	9	0.444	2	8	0.250	25	16		1	10
73	3/6/1967	LAL	W (+2)		9	13	0.692	4	9	0.444	20	11		3	22
74	3/8/1967	BOS	W (+2)	53	8	15	0.533	1	7	0.143	25	3		3	17
75	3/11/1967	BOS	L (-2)		8	17	0.471	5	8	0.625	24	8			21
76	3/12/1967	NYK	W (+11)		6	8	0.750	3	5	0.600	17	6		2	15
77	3/14/1967	SFW	W (+29)	42	9	13	0.692	3	12	0.250	25	9		1	21
78	3/15/1967	LAL	W (+15)		9	15	0.600	3	5	0.600	11	5		1	21
79	3/16/1967	SFW	L (-14)	40	6	18	0.333	4	12	0.333	20	6		3	16
80	3/18/1967	BAL	W (+16)		9	12	0.750	8	12	0.667	17	15		2	26
81	3/19/1967	BAL	W (+3)		16	16	1.000	5	7	0.714	30	4		2	37

1967 Playoffs

G	Date	Opp	W/L	MP	FG	FGA	FG%	FT	FTA	FT%	TRB	AST	BLK	PF	PTS
1	3/21/1967	CIN	L (-4)	48	19	30	0.633	3	9	0.333	22	5		1	41
2	3/22/1967	CIN	W (+21)	48	16	24	0.667	5	9	0.556	27	11		4	37
3	3/24/1967	CIN	W (+15)	48	8	13	0.615	0	2	0.000	30	19		1	16
4	3/25/1967	CIN	W (+18)	48	7	14	0.500	4	13	0.308	27	9		1	18
5	3/31/1967	BOS	W (+14)	48	9	13	0.692	6	10	0.600	32	13	12	3	24
6	4/2/1967	BOS	W (+5)	48	5	11	0.455	5	9	0.556	29	5	5	4	15
7	4/5/1967	BOS	W (+11)	48	8	14	0.571	4	8	0.500	41	9		3	20
8	4/9/1967	BOS	L (-4)	48	8	18	0.444	4	10	0.400	22	10		2	20
9	4/11/1967	BOS	W (+24)	47	10	16	0.625	9	17	0.529	36	13	7	2	29
10	4/14/1967	SFW	W (+6)	53	6	8	0.750	4	9	0.444	33	10	9	2	16
11	4/16/1967	SFW	W (+31)	44	4	10	0.400	2	17	0.118	38	10	10	2	10
12	4/18/1967	SFW	L (-6)	48	12	23	0.522	2	9	0.222	26	5		3	26
13	4/20/1967	SFW	W (+14)	46	3	6	0.500	4	9	0.444	27	8		2	10
14	4/23/1967	SFW	L (-8)	48	9	15	0.600	2	12	0.167	24	4		4	20
15	4/24/1967	SFW	W (+3)	48	8	13	0.615	8	16	0.500	23	4		3	24

G	Date	Opp	W/L	MP	FG	FGA	FG%	FT	FTA	FT%	TRB	AST	BLK	PF	PTS
1	10/18/1967	LAL	W (+16)	48	5	9	0.556	1	7	0.143	30	9		2	11
2	10/21/1967	DET	W (+5)	48	8	13	0.615	1	7	0.143	22	10		2	17
3	10/24/1967	DET	W (+22)	41	4	11	0.364	3	8	0.375	27	5		1	11
4	10/25/1967	NYK	W (+3)	48	8	16	0.500	3	9	0.333	26	6		0	19
5	10/27/1967	SEA	W (+17)	37	6	7	0.857	3	8	0.375	18	9		0	15
6	10/28/1967	BOS	L (-9)	48	7	14	0.500	2	16	0.125	27	9		0	16
7	11/1/1967	BAL	W (+25)	44	8	11	0.727	3	9	0.333	22	13		2	19
8	11/4/1967	SFW	W (+7)	44	0	0		1	2	0.500	18	13		2	1
9	11/7/1967	SDR	W (+25)	38	8	12	0.667	3	6	0.500	11	5		0	19
10	11/8/1967	SDR	W (+15)	44	7	13	0.538	7	15	0.467	24	8		2	21
11	11/10/1967	SFW	L (-19)	44	8	18	0.444	4	7	0.571	27	4		2	20
12	11/11/1967	LAL	W (+4)	48	6	6	1.000	4	6	0.667	28	12		2	16
13	11/14/1967	CIN	W (+20)	41	12	14	0.857	3	6	0.500	26	9		3	27
14	11/15/1967	DET	L (-3)	48	4	12	0.333	4	10	0.400	20	9		4	12
15	11/17/1967	STL	W (+8)	44	4	12	0.333	3	9	0.333	24	7		1	11
16	11/18/1967	BOS	L (-5)	48	3	11	0.273	2	7	0.286	33	6		3	8
17	11/22/1967	STL	L (-2)	48	4	9	0.444	4	11	0.364	23	6		3	12
18	11/23/1967	SDR	W (+11)	45	13	23	0.565	5	13	0.385	27	6		1	31
19	11/24/1967	CHI	W (+18)	45	16	23	0.696	2	9	0.222	29	3		1	34
20	11/25/1967	CHI	L (-5)	48	10	17	0.588	4	19	0.211	22	7		1	24
21	11/28/1967	NYK	W (+2)	44	3	12	0.250	4	8	0.500	19	6		1	10

G	Date	Opp	W/L	MP	FG	FGA	FG%	FT	FTA	FT%	TRB	AST	BLK	PF	PTS
22	11/29/1967	SFW	L (-18)	45	3	11	0.273	6	17	0.353	23	4		3	12
23	12/1/1967	SEA	W (+24)	48	22	29	0.759	8	30	0.267	37	2		3	52
24	12/2/1967	BAL	W (+9)	47	11	19	0.579	5	18	0.278	16	8		1	27
25	12/5/1967	LAL	L (-6)	53	12	28	0.429	7	15	0.467	31	5		1	31
26	12/6/1967	CIN	W (+1)	48	11	23	0.478	7	13	0.538	19	3		3	29
27	12/8/1967	NYK	W (+8)	48	10	22	0.455	6	11	0.545	21	5		3	26
28	12/9/1967	BAL	W (+14)	46	5	9	0.556	5	11	0.455	24	10		3	15
29	12/12/1967	SEA	W (+11)	48	4	13	0.308	6	25	0.240	27	5		1	14
30	12/14/1967	BOS	L (-1)	47	4	14	0.286	2	8	0.250	23	5		1	10
31	12/15/1967	STL	W (+9)	48	8	15	0.533	7	8	0.875	19	5		4	23
32	12/16/1967	CHI	W (+20)	48	30	40	0.750	8	22	0.364	34	2		1	68
33	12/17/1967	SEA	W (+15)	48	19	24	0.792	9	17	0.529	26	4		4	47
34	12/20/1967	SEA	W (+38)	45	20	23	0.870	13	26	0.500	38	6		2	53
35	12/25/1967	BAL	W (+3)	48	6	10	0.600	3	9	0.333	25	4		2	15
36	12/26/1967	CIN	W (+5)	48	8	16	0.500	4	10	0.400	26	10		3	20
37	12/27/1967	NYK	W (+9)	48	11	19	0.579	5	15	0.333	21	3		2	27
38	12/29/1967	BOS	W (+10)	48	13	23	0.565	5	15	0.333	27	6		4	31
39	12/30/1967	DET	W (+15)	48	12	22	0.545	6	13	0.462	18	6		1	30
40	1/3/1968	NYK	L (-14)	48	17	26	0.654	5	8	0.625	20	6		2	39
41	1/5/1968	LAL	W (+12)	48	16	27	0.593	3	12	0.250	24	6		2	35
42	1/6/1968	STL	W (+11)	48	10	20	0.500	6	17	0.353	23	10		2	26

G	Date	Opp	W/L	MP	FG	FGA	FG%	FT	FTA	FT%	TRB	AST	BLK	PF	PTS
43	1/7/1968	CIN	L (-16)	48	16	33	0.485	4	10	0.400	25	7		4	36
44	1/10/1968	STL	L (-12)	47	14	21	0.667	4	13	0.308	16	5		2	32
45	1/12/1968	BAL	W (+17)	46	16	25	0.640	4	13	0.308	35	6		2	36
46	1/13/1968	DET	W (+9)	48	10	20	0.500	7	10	0.700	20	10		5	27
47	1/17/1968	LAL	L (-9)	48	6	11	0.545	7	20	0.350	20	7		0	19
48	1/19/1968	SFW	L (-11)	48	8	18	0.444	4	19	0.211	27	7		1	20
49	1/20/1968	CHI	W (+24)	46	8	10	0.800	2	8	0.250	21	8		0	18
50	1/25/1968	DET	W (+15)	48	7	11	0.636	0	4	0.000	11	14		3	14
51	1/26/1968	CIN	W (+10)	48	10	14	0.714	2	8	0.250	22	12		2	22
52	1/28/1968	BOS	L (-12)	48	9	17	0.529	1	8	0.125	24	11		0	19
53	1/30/1968	BOS	W (+7)	48	8	14	0.571	7	13	0.538	29	13		0	23
54	2/2/1968	DET	W (+10)	48	9	13	0.692	4	12	0.333	25	21		0	22
55	2/3/1968	BAL	W (+12)	48	10	13	0.769	5	6	0.833	26	7		1	25
56	2/4/1968	SFW	W (+24)	45	6	12	0.500	7	19	0.368	27	16		1	19
57	2/7/1968	SDR	W (+22)	46	9	12	0.750	3	12	0.250	21	14		2	21
58	2/9/1968	CHI	W (+5)	48	8	11	0.727	4	12	0.333	17	11		3	20
59	2/10/1968	NYK	L (-18)	46	8	18	0.444	0	3	0.000	12	7		2	16
60	2/11/1968	STL	W (+26)	45	10	16	0.625	1	6	0.167	26	13		1	21
61	2/13/1968	SFW	W (+7)	48	6	12	0.500	4	10	0.400	25	14		4	16
62	2/14/1968	SEA	W (+24)	44	15	18	0.833	5	12	0.417	24	15		2	35
63	2/16/1968	SDR	W (+16)	46	9	13	0.692	2	8	0.250	19	13		1	20

G	Date	Opp	W/L	MP	FG	FGA	FG%	FT	FTA	FT%	TRB	AST	BLK	PF	PTS
64	2/17/1968	LAL	W (+1)	58	14	20	0.700	4	7	0.571	23	7		3	32
65	2/18/1968	SDR	L (-5)	48	12	23	0.522	10	21	0.476	27	4		2	34
66	2/20/1968	SEA	W (+32)	45	9	21	0.429	2	10	0.200	20	7		0	20
67	2/23/1968	DET	W (+21)	48	12	20	0.600	7	16	0.438	32	12		2	31
68	2/25/1968	STL	W (+7)	48	14	22	0.636	3	10	0.300	19	4		2	31
69	2/27/1968	SFW	W (+20)	45	15	25	0.600	3	10	0.300	31	5		4	33
70	3/3/1968	BOS	W (+6)	48	6	13	0.462	5	10	0.500	22	8		4	17
71	3/5/1968	SDR	W (+31)	43	12	20	0.600	7	14	0.500	21	15		2	31
72	3/6/1968	CIN	L (-2)	48	8	14	0.571	6	11	0.545	19	13		3	22
73	3/7/1968	CIN	W (+8)	48	16	21	0.762	6	10	0.600	28	9		0	38
74	3/8/1968	BOS	W (+5)	48	5	10	0.500	3	6	0.500	24	10		1	13
75	3/10/1968	NYK	W (+11)	48	11	15	0.733	6	12	0.500	27	10		4	28
76	3/12/1968	CHI	W (+24)	46	9	12	0.750	4	8	0.500	30	12		3	22
77	3/13/1968	NYK	L (-10)	48	7	10	0.700	2	6	0.333	20	10		2	16
78	3/15/1968	BAL	W (+7)	48	11	15	0.733	3	8	0.375	21	13		3	25
79	3/16/1968	CHI	W (+22)	46	16	18	0.889	3	8	0.375	15	10		4	35
80	3/18/1968	LAL	W (+30)	48	24	29	0.828	5	10	0.500	32	14		0	53
81	3/19/1968	CIN	L (-1)	53	10	22	0.455	2	10	0.200	27	19		1	22
82	3/20/1968	BAL	W (+18)	45	11	19	0.579	4	10	0.400	17	12		2	26

1968 Playoffs

G	Date	Opp	W/L	MP	FG	FGA	FG%	FT	FTA	FT%	TRB	AST	BLK	PF	PTS
1	3/22/1968	NYK	W (+8)	48	17	29	0.586	3	5	0.600	29	7		2	37
2	3/23/1968	NYK	L (-11)	48	11	21	0.524	2	4	0.500	17	8		2	24
3	3/27/1968	NYK	W (+6)	58	8	10	0.800	2	13	0.154	24	8		3	18
4	3/30/1968	NYK	L (-9)	48	9	18	0.500	5	17	0.294	27	5		3	23
5	3/31/1968	NYK	W (+18)	46	11	16	0.688	4	13	0.308	21	7		1	26
6	4/1/1968	NYK	W (+16)	48	10	19	0.526	5	15	0.333	27	3		5	25
7	4/5/1968	BOS	L (-9)	48	14	24	0.583	5	11	0.455	25	5		1	33
8	4/10/1968	BOS	W (+9)	48	6	14	0.429	3	6	0.500	19	8		2	15
9	4/11/1968	BOS	W (+8)	47	10	19	0.526	3	12	0.250	25	6		3	23
10	4/14/1968	BOS	W (+5)	48	7	11	0.636	8	15	0.533	16	8		5	22
11	4/15/1968	BOS	L (-18)	48	11	21	0.524	6	11	0.545	30	7		0	28
12	4/17/1968	BOS	L (-8)	48	6	21	0.286	8	22	0.364	27	8		1	20
13	4/19/1968	BOS	L (-4)	48	4	9	0.444	6	15	0.400	34	5		2	14

Game Logs 1968-69

G	Date	Opp	W/L	MP	FG	FGA	FG%	FT	FTA	FT%	TRB	AST	BLK	PF	PTS
1	10/18/1968	PHI	L (-18)	34	5	7	0.714	5	11	0.455	17	5		1	15
2	10/19/1968	NYK	W (+22)	37	13	15	0.867	3	11	0.273	23	6		2	29
3	10/22/1968	CIN	L (-4)		8	15	0.533	3	6	0.500	32			1	19
4	10/23/1968	DET	L (-7)		12			5	15	0.333	21	4			29
5	10/25/1968	BAL	W (+6)	48	11	14	0.786	2	8	0.250	21	2		1	24
6	10/27/1968	SDR	W (+36)		11	18	0.611	6	13	0.462	23	1		1	28
7	10/29/1968	ATL	W (+1)		10	16	0.625	5	12	0.417	18	1		2	25
8	11/1/1968	CHI	L (-13)	40	11	15	0.733	7	13	0.538	18	2		2	29
9	11/5/1968	CHI	W (+3)		8			8	17	0.471	21				24
10	11/6/1968	MIL	W (+13)		10			3	7	0.429	20	9			23
11	11/8/1968	NYK	W (+2)	44	6	8	0.750	1	5	0.200	19	4		5	13
12	11/10/1968	NYK	W (+21)	42	8	11	0.727	5	10	0.500	21	7		1	21
13	11/15/1968	SDR	W (+8)		8	12	0.667	5	12	0.417	20	7		1	21
14	11/16/1968	SFW	W (+7)	48	6	12	0.500	3	8	0.375	23	5		3	15
15	11/17/1968	SEA	W (+11)		7	11	0.636	3	17	0.176	24	2		2	17
16	11/19/1968	BOS	W (+10)		6	11	0.545	4	8	0.500	22	4		2	16
17	11/22/1968	SFW	L (-2)	48	7	10	0.700	6	11	0.545	16	3		4	20
18	11/24/1968	CHI	W (+3)		1	5	0.200	4	14	0.286	18	2		0	6
19	11/26/1968	NYK	L (-4)	46	11	15	0.733	1	4	0.250	27	3		4	23
20	11/28/1968	PHI	L (-15)	41	5	11	0.455	3	9	0.333	19	5		2	13
21	11/29/1968	BOS	W (+1)	48	6	14	0.429	2	4	0.500	22	4		1	14

G	Date	Opp	W/L	MP	FG	FGA	FG%	FT	FTA	FT%	TRB	AST	BLK	PF	PTS
22	12/1/1968	MIL	W (+7)		2	7	0.286	5	12	0.417	27	9		3	9
23	12/3/1968	PHO	W (+14)	38	12	20	0.600	11	15	0.733	25	3		1	35
24	12/5/1968	BAL	L (-18)		7			3	7	0.429					17
25	12/6/1968	ATL	W (+5)	48	8	12	0.667	4	10	0.400	16	1		2	20
26	12/7/1968	CHI	L (-9)		7			6	22	0.273	23				20
27	12/8/1968	SDR	W (+14)	41	13	23	0.565	9	18	0.500	23	4		1	35
28	12/13/1968	ATL	L (-2)	48	8	16	0.500	6	15	0.400	22	3		2	22
29	12/14/1968	SEA	W (+16)		9	20	0.450	4	9	0.444	15	3			22
30	12/15/1968	SEA	W (+1)	38	5	11	0.455	2	10	0.200	20	5		3	12
31	12/17/1968	CIN	W (+4)		1	3	0.333	0	6	0.000	21	5		2	2
32	12/20/1968	SFW	W (+32)	30	2	7	0.286	1	3	0.333	18	4		2	5
33	12/22/1968	PHI	W (+3)	48	6	14	0.429	4	7	0.571	22	4	4	1	16
34	12/25/1968	PHO	W (+20)	42	6	8	0.750	3	9	0.333	15	6	23	3	15
35	12/26/1968	DET	W (+1)		8			1	5	0.200	24				17
36	12/28/1968	CHI	L (-7)		5			4	8	0.500	19				14
37	12/29/1968	DET	W (+3)		10	16	0.625	2	7	0.286	25	6		1	22
38	12/30/1968	SDR	W (+5)	47	10	18	0.556	5	13	0.385	23	8		4	25
39	12/31/1968	DET	L (-20)		11	15	0.733	3	7	0.429	11	5		4	25
40	1/3/1969	PHI	L (-29)	31	3	6	0.500	2	11	0.182	7	7	1	1	8
41	1/4/1969	ATL	W (+10)	48	2	8	0.250	3	4	0.750	20	2		5	7
42	1/7/1969	BAL	W (+7)		5			5	11	0.455					15

G	Date	Opp	W/L	MP	FG	FGA	FG%	FT	FTA	FT%	TRB	AST	BLK	PF	PTS
43	1/10/1969	BOS	L (-6)		4	10	0.400	2	5	0.400	18	4		0	10
44	1/11/1969	ATL	L (-4)	48	6	15	0.400	9	15	0.600	17	2		1	21
45	1/17/1969	CIN	W (+21)		12	16	0.750	3	10	0.300	25	7	12	1	27
46	1/19/1969	CIN	W (+15)		6	13	0.462	3	6	0.500	21	3	9	1	15
47	1/21/1969	MIL	W (+17)		2	6	0.333	0	0		20		6	1	4
48	1/22/1969	DET	L (-1)		10			5	6	0.833	25				25
49	1/24/1969	ATL	L (-4)		4	11	0.364	3	8	0.375	10	5		1	11
50	1/26/1969	CIN	W (+13)		22	36	0.611	16	24	0.667	21			1	60
51	1/28/1969	CHI	W (+7)		9	16	0.563	8	17	0.471	13	5		0	26
52	1/29/1969	SDR	W (+2)		10	19	0.526	10	16	0.625	25	6		2	30
53	1/31/1969	MIL	W (+1)		7	14	0.500	5	15	0.333	25	4	20?	1	19
54	2/1/1969	SFW	W (+5)	53	4	9	0.444	3	5	0.600	30	3		2	11
55	2/2/1969	SFW	L (-5)	63	7	10	0.700	9	17	0.529	35	3		5	23
56	2/3/1969	SEA	L (-7)	46	11	24	0.458	11	23	0.478	17	3		0	33
57	2/7/1969	PHI	L (-3)		8	14	0.571	2	7	0.286	22	3		1	18
58	2/8/1969	PHO	W (+18)	45	11	22	0.500	1	4	0.250	22	10		0	23
59	2/9/1969	PHO	W (+18)	48	29	35	0.829	8	18	0.444	27	4		1	66
60	2/12/1969	SEA	W (+17)	48	10	19	0.526	12	21	0.571	33	2		1	32
61	2/14/1969	SDR	W (+6)		7	13	0.538	11	19	0.579	16	8		4	25
62	2/16/1969	MIL	L (-9)		11	21	0.524	7	15	0.467	22	4		2	29
63	2/18/1969	NYK	W (+4)	48	11	17	0.647	9	17	0.529	23	2		3	31

G	Date	Opp	W/L	MP	FG	FGA	FG%	FT	FTA	FT%	TRB	AST	BLK	PF	PTS
64	2/19/1969	BAL	L (-22)	43	10	20	0.500	6	14	0.429	21	2		2	26
65	2/21/1969	BOS	L (-22)		13	22	0.591	9	21	0.429	19	6		1	35
66	2/23/1969	PHI	L (-4)	46	14	21	0.667	8	13	0.615	16	1		2	36
67	2/25/1969	SEA	W (+3)		3	8	0.375	8	21	0.381	23	6		4	14
68	2/28/1969	PHO	W (+4)	36	6	15	0.400	5	7	0.714	15	2		1	17
69	3/1/1969	SDR	W (+6)	45	5	8	0.625	5	11	0.455	11	11		4	15
70	3/2/1969	SFW	W (+15)	42	3	7	0.429	3	4	0.750	18	6		0	9
71	3/4/1969	BAL	L (-8)	38	9	16	0.563	4	7	0.571	14	0		1	22
72	3/7/1969	BOS	W (+6)	53	3	8	0.375	6	12	0.500	42	6		2	12
73	3/9/1969	BAL	W (+11)		12	16	0.750	1	8	0.125	38	7		4	25
74	3/11/1969	DET	W (+36)	40	14	14	1.000	6	9	0.667	27	7	11	2	34
75	3/12/1969	SFW	L (-12)	48	2	5	0.400	1	2	0.500	20	2		1	5
76	3/14/1969	MIL	W (+8)		6	9	0.667	3	5	0.600	20	11		1	15
77	3/16/1969	BOS	W (+35)	42	4	6	0.667	3	8	0.375	21	5	6	2	11
78	3/18/1969	CHI	W (+1)		4			1	6	0.167	15			0	9
79	3/19/1969	CIN	L (-8)		3	11	0.273	3	5	0.600	16			3	9
80	3/21/1969	ATL	W (+13)		8	10	0.800	3	8	0.375	28	6		0	19
81	3/23/1969	NYK	W (+17)	48	11	15	0.733	3	4	0.750	21	6		5	25

G	Date	Opp	W/L	MP	FG	FGA	FG%	FT	FTA	FT%	TRB	AST	BLK	PF	PTS
1	3/26/1969	SFW	L (-5)		5	11	0.455	1	3	0.333	30	3		4	11
2	3/28/1969	SFW	L (-6)		4	10	0.400	2	9	0.222	17	1		5	10
3	3/31/1969	SFW	W (+17)		9	14	0.643	4	13	0.308	28	5		4	22
4	4/2/1969	SFW	W (+15)		4	10	0.400	3	6	0.500	14	3	9	1	11
5	4/4/1969	SFW	W (+5)		3	6	0.500	1	3	0.333	27	2	10	3	7
6	4/5/1969	SFW	W (+40)		5	9	0.556	1	3	0.333	25	1		2	11
7	4/11/1969	ATL	W (+2)		6	8	0.750	3	11	0.273	29	2		5	15
8	4/13/1969	ATL	W (+2)		10	14	0.714	3	7	0.429	29	1		4	23
9	4/15/1969	ATL	L (-13)		7	16	0.438	3	4	0.750	22	2		1	17
10	4/17/1969	ATL	W (+15)		9	9	1.000	7	12	0.583	19	2		3	25
11	4/20/1969	ATL	W (+8)		5	11	0.455	6	13	0.462	29	3	16	3	16
12	4/23/1969	BOS	W (+2)	48	6	11	0.545	3	9	0.333	23	4	12	4	15
13	4/25/1969	BOS	W (+6)	48	1	6	0.167	2	4	0.500	19	4		3	4
14	4/27/1969	BOS	L (-6)	48	6	11	0.545	4	11	0.364	26	2		3	16
15	4/29/1969	BOS	L (-1)	48	3	8	0.375	2	11	0.182	31	1		3	8
16	5/1/1969	BOS	W (+13)	48	5	9	0.556	3	8	0.375	31	3		0	13
17	5/3/1969	BOS	L (-9)	48	1	5	0.200	6	10	0.600	18	4		3	8
18	5/5/1969	BOS	L (-2)	43	7	8	0.875	4	13	0.308	27	3		5	18

G	Date	Opp	W/L	MP	FG	FGA	FG%	FT	FTA	FT%	TRB	AST	BLK	PF	PTS
1	10/17/1969	PHI	L (-5)		10			15	30	0.500					35
2	10/18/1969	NYK	L (-3)		5			2	8	0.250					12
3	10/21/1969	BAL	W (+5)		16			6	12	0.500					38
4	10/22/1969	CIN	W (+7)		17			9	21	0.429					43
5	10/24/1969	MIL	W (+11)		9			7	18	0.389			3		25
6	10/25/1969	SEA	W (+24)		19			4	10	0.400					42
7	10/26/1969	CHI	W (+4)		14			9	19	0.474					37
8	11/2/1969	CIN	L (-8)		10			5	9	0.556					25
9	11/7/1969	PHO	L (-2)	28	13	14	0.929	7	13	0.538	15	2		2	33
10	3/18/1970	BOS	L (-15)		6			3	7	0.429					15
11	3/20/1970	DET	W (+6)		1			0	1	0.000					2
12	3/22/1970	SEA	W (+3)		9			3	9	0.333					21

G	Date	Opp	W/L	MP	FG	FGA	FG%	FT	FTA	FT%	TRB	AST	BLK	PF	PTS
1	3/25/1970	PHO	W (+16)	45	12	19	0.632	5	10	0.500	19	5		1	29
2	3/29/1970	PHO	L (-13)	48	6	17	0.353	7	16	0.438	25	4		2	19
3	4/2/1970	PHO	L (-14)	45	5	8	0.625	1	2	0.500	12	7		1	11
4	4/4/1970	PHO	L (-10)	48	12	20	0.600	5	17	0.294	19	0		1	29
5	4/5/1970	PHO	W (+17)	46	12	20	0.600	12	19	0.632	14	3	10	2	36
6	4/7/1970	PHO	W (+11)	48	4	11	0.364	4	12	0.333	26	11	12	1	12
7	4/9/1970	PHO	W (+35)	43	11	18	0.611	8	17	0.471	27	6	11	2	30
8	4/12/1970	ATL	W (+4)	48	6	12	0.500	4	10	0.400	17	8		2	16
9	4/14/1970	ATL	W (+11)	48	10	23	0.435	4	7	0.571	24	4		4	24
10	4/17/1970	ATL	W (+1)	53	5	13	0.385	8	17	0.471	26	2		5	18
11	4/19/1970	ATL	W (+19)	46	5	10	0.500	1	8	0.125	21	3	10	3	11
12	4/24/1970	NYK	L (-12)	48	8	14	0.571	1	10	0.100	24	5		2	17
13	4/27/1970	NYK	W (+2)	44	9	20	0.450	1	3	0.333	24	2		3	19
14	4/29/1970	NYK	L (-3)	53	7	10	0.700	7	13	0.538	26	4		4	21
15	5/1/1970	NYK	W (+6)	49	7	13	0.538	4	7	0.571	25	7		3	18
16	5/4/1970	NYK	L (-7)	45	9	12	0.750	4	9	0.444	19	3		2	22
17	5/6/1970	NYK	W (+22)	46	20	27	0.741	5	14	0.357	27	3		3	45
18	5/8/1970	NYK	L (-14)	48	10	16	0.625	1	11	0.091	24	4	2	1	21

G	Date	Opp	W/L	MP	FG	FGA	FG%	FT	FTA	FT%	TRB	AST	BLK	PF	PTS
1	10/16/1970	CHI	W (+4)	48	10	18	0.556	6	16	0.375	31	7		2	26
2	10/17/1970	BAL	L (-2)		10			3	7	0.429					23
3	10/20/1970	NYK	L (-15)	48	9	18	0.500	2	6	0.333	18	0		1	20
4	10/21/1970	PHI	W (+24)	45	9	12	0.750	8	13	0.615	22	1		2	26
5	10/23/1970	PHI	L (-5)	48	14	23	0.609	6	12	0.500	21	6		4	34
6	10/25/1970	CLE	W (+27)	44	10	21	0.476	4	9	0.444	25	3		0	24
7	10/30/1970	BUF	W (+14)	46	8	14	0.571	4	12	0.333	16	5		4	20
8	11/3/1970	POR	W (+20)	42	8	15	0.533	7	15	0.467	15	0		0	23
9	11/6/1970	NYK	W (+2)	45	3	6	0.500	2	7	0.286	16	3		4	8
10	11/8/1970	BAL	W (+19)	45	10	15	0.667	0	2	0.000	24	6		2	20
11	11/10/1970	CHI	L (-22)	48	8	14	0.571	3	5	0.600	24	4		4	19
12	11/11/1970	DET	W (+2)	48	10	14	0.714	7	13	0.538	12	3		3	27
13	11/13/1970	DET	W (+13)	47	10	17	0.588	4	8	0.500	18	3		2	24
14	11/17/1970	ATL	W (+11)	48	11	24	0.458	2	4	0.500	23	3		2	24
15	11/19/1970	SEA	L (-1)		12			8	10	0.800					32
16	11/20/1970	MIL	L (-17)	48	7	20	0.350	14	16	0.875	23	3	10	4	28
17	11/22/1970	SEA	W (+25)	42	10	17	0.588	11	15	0.733	21	3		1	31
18	11/27/1970	PHO	L (-11)	48	4	10	0.400	4	6	0.667	13	2		3	12
19	11/28/1970	SFW	L (-4)	48	4	7	0.571	4	7	0.571	14	1		1	12
20	11/29/1970	SDR	W (+18)	46	7	14	0.500	5	7	0.714	31	7		4	19
21	12/1/1970	BAL	W (+4)	48	9	14	0.643	0	4	0.000	17	2		0	18

G	Date	Opp	W/L	MP	FG	FGA	FG%	FT	FTA	FT%	TRB	AST	BLK	PF	PTS
22	12/2/1970	BOS	L (-3)	48	9	13	0.692	11	14	0.786	14	1		0	29
23	12/4/1970	SFW	W (+22)	40	2	2	1.000	1	4	0.250	17	6		2	5
24	12/5/1970	SDR	L (-3)	48	15	27	0.556	6	11	0.545	14	2		1	36
25	12/6/1970	POR	W (+11)	48	14	20	0.700	3	8	0.375	18	3		2	31
26	12/8/1970	PHO	W (+9)	48	14	22	0.636	8	9	0.889	16	7		2	36
27	12/11/1970	SEA	W (+8)	45	9	19	0.474	4	8	0.500	25	11		2	22
28	12/13/1970	DET	L (-3)	48	6	15	0.400	0	6	0.000	25	8		2	12
29	12/15/1970	BUF	L (-2)		10			5	8	0.625					25
30	12/16/1970	CIN	W (+16)	45	14	26	0.538	7	11	0.636	18	6		1	35
31	12/19/1970	ATL	W (+12)	46	8	18	0.444	4	9	0.444	21	5		2	20
32	12/21/1970	MIL	L (-25)	45	11	23	0.478	3	7	0.429	14	4	2	4	25
33	12/22/1970	ATL	L (-4)	48	7	13	0.538	4	6	0.667	27	2		1	18
34	12/25/1970	BOS	W (+10)	37	8	12	0.667	8	19	0.421	22	4		0	24
35	12/27/1970	PHO	W (+18)	45	12	18	0.667	4	12	0.333	9	5		4	28
36	12/29/1970	CHI	W (+9)	46	14	22	0.636	6	13	0.462	16	3		2	34
37	12/30/1970	PHO	L (-18)	46	10	21	0.476	12	17	0.706	10	4		1	32
38	1/1/1971	SDR	L (-11)	45	4	13	0.308	1	4	0.250	19	2		4	9
39	1/2/1971	SDR	L (-1)		9			7	14	0.500					25
40	1/5/1971	CIN	L (-34)		17	26	0.654	7	19	0.368	23			1	41
41	1/7/1971	CLE	W (+5)	44	6	12	0.500	0	0		12	5		2	12
42	1/8/1971	PHI	W (+6)	44	8	12	0.667	4	10	0.400	17	4	6	5	20

G	Date	Opp	W/L	MP	FG	FGA	FG%	FT	FTA	FT%	TRB	AST	BLK	PF	PTS
43	1/10/1971	DET	L (-9)	48	12	18	0.667	1	8	0.125	16	6		3	25
44	1/14/1971	CIN	W (+6)		14	20	0.700	2	3	0.667	15			2	30
45	1/16/1971	ATL	L (-4)	48	7	16	0.438	1	3	0.333	13	9		3	15
46	1/19/1971	PHI	W (+20)	36	1	5	0.200	1	5	0.200	16	1		1	3
47	1/22/1971	SFW	W (+20)	41	6	9	0.667	0	3	0.000	20	7		4	12
48	1/24/1971	CIN	W (+11)	48	15	23	0.652	5	8	0.625	29	7		2	35
49	1/26/1971	CHI	W (+25)	39	4	10	0.400	3	4	0.750	14	10		1	11
50	1/28/1971	PHO	L (-6)	47	7	15	0.467	10	15	0.667	23	2			24
51	1/29/1971	SEA	W (+7)		12			3	6	0.500					27
52	1/30/1971	SFW	L (-2)	48	6	14	0.429	1	2	0.500	22	5		1	13
53	1/31/1971	POR	W (+13)	43	11	22	0.500	11	18	0.611	27	6		1	33
54	2/2/1971	SDR	W (+28)	37	3	6	0.500	3	4	0.750	10	5		1	9
55	2/5/1971	MIL	W (+23)	40	7	10	0.700	0	2	0.000	14	3	6	4	14
56	2/6/1971	SDR	W (+7)		6			4	9	0.444					16
57	2/7/1971	SFW	W (+15)		4			1	2	0.500					9
58	2/9/1971	CLE	W (+5)	48	5	15	0.333	1	2	0.500	19	4		2	11
59	2/11/1971	MIL	L (-34)	36	10	19	0.526	5	6	0.833	11	1		2	25
60	2/12/1971	CHI	L (-19)	48	7	13	0.538	3	7	0.429	14	3		4	17
61	2/14/1971	CIN	W (+12)	29	4	16	0.250	3	4	0.750	4	3		3	11
62	2/16/1971	NYK	W (+15)	44	8	10	0.800	3	7	0.429	21	2		2	19
63	2/18/1971	POR	W (+22)	35	9	14	0.643	0	0		14	8		1	18

G	Date	Opp	W/L	MP	FG	FGA	FG%	FT	FTA	FT%	TRB	AST	BLK	PF	PTS
64	2/19/1971	PHI	L (-14)	45	1	5	0.200	3	7	0.429	14	1		4	5
65	2/21/1971	BOS	W (+8)		10			5	9	0.556					25
66	2/23/1971	BAL	W (+7)	48	4	10	0.400	3	6	0.500	18	3		3	11
67	2/24/1971	BOS	L (-20)		8			11	16	0.688					27
68	2/26/1971	SEA	W (+24)	43	10	13	0.769	10	16	0.625	19	5		1	30
69	2/27/1971	SFW	W (+5)	48	4	5	0.800	2	3	0.667	13	9		1	10
70	2/28/1971	CLE	W (+17)	37	3	7	0.429	1	4	0.250	18	2		0	7
71	3/2/1971	BUF	W (+13)		8			2	2	1.000					18
72	3/3/1971	MIL	L (-15)		7			10	12	0.833			8		24
73	3/5/1971	ATL	L (-1)	48	10	26	0.385	2	5	0.400	28	6		4	22
74	3/6/1971	SEA	L (-12)	46	6	15	0.400	10	16	0.625	11	4		3	22
75	3/7/1971	CHI	W (+9)	48	8	18	0.444	4	10	0.400	32	5		4	20
76	3/9/1971	BAL	L (-12)	44	12	18	0.667	4	7	0.571	20	4		0	28
77	3/12/1971	BUF	L (-7)	24	3	5	0.600	1	1	1.000	9	4		1	7
78	3/14/1971	DET	W (+10)	31	4	4	1.000	3	5	0.600	16	5		1	11
79	3/16/1971	NYK	L (-33)	38	3	5	0.600	2	4	0.500	14	1		1	8
80	3/17/1971	BOS	L (-8)	41	9	21	0.429	7	9	0.778	15	4		2	25
81	3/19/1971	PHO	L (-5)	48	9	18	0.500	10	16	0.625	21	6	12		28
82	3/21/1971	NYK	W (+3)	12	1	2	0.500	0	1	0.000	7	1		0	2

1971 Playoffs

G	Date	Opp	W/L	MP	FG	FGA	FG%	FT	FTA	FT%	TRB	AST	BLK	PF	PTS
1	3/24/1971	CHI	W (+1)	48	6	18	0.333	6	9	0.667	21	3		4	18
2	3/26/1971	CHI	W (+10)	48	11	19	0.579	4	8	0.500	20	2		2	26
3	3/28/1971	CHI	L (-8)	48	3	11	0.273	2	4	0.500	18	6		3	8
4	3/30/1971	CHI	L (-10)	47	4	13	0.308	4	5	0.800	23	7	10	0	12
5	4/1/1971	CHI	W (+26)	45	4	9	0.444	0	2	0.000	14	7		3	8
6	4/4/1971	CHI	L (-14)	48	4	10	0.400	5	10	0.500	33	9	4	3	13
7	4/6/1971	CHI	W (+11)	48	7	12	0.583	11	17	0.647	19	9		4	25
8	4/9/1971	MIL	L (-21)	46	10	19	0.526	2	10	0.200	20	1	8	3	22
9	4/11/1971	MIL	L (-18)	48	10	21	0.476	6	8	0.750	22	0		1	26
10	4/14/1971	MIL	W (+11)	48	9	19	0.474	6	12	0.500	24	3	3	2	24
11	4/16/1971	MIL	L (-23)		7	14	0.500	1	3	0.333	16	2	6	3	15
12	4/18/1971	MIL	L (-18)	46	10	21	0.476	3	9	0.333	12	4		5	23

Game Logs 1971-72

G	Date	Opp	W/L	MP	FG	FGA	FG%	FT	FTA	FT%	TRB	AST	BLK	PF	PTS
1	10/15/1971	DET	W (+29)	35	11	14	0.786	4	5	0.800	15	5		4	26
2	10/16/1971	NYK	W (+15)	41	6	14	0.429	3	8	0.375	19	2		1	15
3	10/19/1971	BUF	W (+17)		9			2	13	0.154					20
4	10/20/1971	ATL	W (+22)	42	8	14	0.571	2	5	0.400	25	2		4	18
5	10/22/1971	CHI	L (-7)	35	2	5	0.400	0	4	0.000	18	1		3	4
6	10/24/1971	HOU	W (+10)	40	8	13	0.615	1	10	0.100	13	3		0	17
7	10/29/1971	CIN	W (+12)	40	10	18	0.556	5	19	0.263	32	4		2	25
8	10/30/1971	SEA	L (-9)	40	3	5	0.600	1	6	0.167	11	2		2	7
9	10/31/1971	GSW	L (-4)	44	6	11	0.545	0	2	0.000	24	6		1	12
10	11/5/1971	BAL	W (+4)	41	6	13	0.462	0	1	0.000	25	6		1	12
11	11/6/1971	GSW	W (+16)		2			0	0						4
12	11/7/1971	NYK	W (+7)	42	5	8	0.625	0	5	0.000	20	7	6	2	10
13	11/9/1971	CHI	W (+13)	41	2	6	0.333	1	3	0.333	14	8		2	5
14	11/10/1971	PHI	W (+40)	36	3	7	0.429	0	1	0.000	22	1	8	3	6
15	11/12/1971	SEA	W (+8)	42	2	2	1.000	3	6	0.500	13	3		3	7
16	11/13/1971	POR	W (+22)	29	3	5	0.600	0	2	0.000	31	5		0	6
17	11/14/1971	BOS	W (+13)	45	1	2	0.500	1	2	0.500	15	10		2	3
18	11/16/1971	CLE	W (+18)	38	2	2	1.000	0	1	0.000	23	6		3	4
19	11/19/1971	HOU	W (+7)	45	6	12	0.500	1	4	0.250	26	6		3	13
20	11/21/1971	MIL	W (+7)	48	4	9	0.444	3	9	0.333	15	6	4	4	11
21	11/25/1971	SEA	W (+24)	36	7	8	0.875	3	5	0.600	15	3	12	2	17

G	Date	Opp	W/L	MP	FG	FGA	FG%	FT	FTA	FT%	TRB	AST	BLK	PF	PTS
22	11/26/1971	DET	W (+19)	43	15	22	0.682	1	5	0.200	31	1	6	1	31
23	11/28/1971	SEA	W (+17)	41	9	12	0.750	3	8	0.375	26	1	5	4	21
24	12/1/1971	BOS	W (+13)	48	2	8	0.250	4	8	0.500	20	6		4	8
25	12/3/1971	PHI	W (+15)	48	2	3	0.667	4	7	0.571	25	3	9	2	8
26	12/5/1971	POR	W (+16)	44	8	10	0.800	1	2	0.500	27	5		2	17
27	12/8/1971	HOU	W (+5)		1			1	3	0.333			7		3
28	12/9/1971	GSW	W (+13)		1			1	1	1.000			12		3
29	12/10/1971	PHO	W (+9)	53	7	8	0.875	0	6	0.000	28	7		4	14
30	12/12/1971	ATL	W (+9)	48	3	6	0.500	2	2	1.000	24	4	6	3	8
31	12/14/1971	POR	W (+15)	45	9	10	0.900	6	10	0.600	18	8	7	1	24
32	12/17/1971	GSW	W (+30)	41	3	3	1.000	1	1	1.000	18	2	6	3	7
33	12/18/1971	PHO	W (+26)	45	7	11	0.636	4	13	0.308	16	4	5	4	18
34	12/19/1971	PHI	W (+22)	43	12	15	0.800	8	13	0.615	34	4	12	3	32
35	12/21/1971	BUF	W (+14)	48	12	15	0.800	7	12	0.583	22	2	11	4	31
36	12/22/1971	BAL	W (+7)	44	2	4	0.500	2	3	0.667	14	5		3	6
37	12/26/1971	HOU	W (+22)	43	7	10	0.700	0	2	0.000	13	3		4	14
38	12/28/1971	BUF	W (+18)	43	9	10	0.900	5	11	0.455	13	5		1	23
39	12/30/1971	SEA	W (+16)		8			1	7	0.143			8		17
40	1/2/1972	BOS	W (+9)	45	0	3	0.000	4	7	0.571	17	2		3	4
41	1/5/1972	CLE	W (+10)	43	4	7	0.571	2	5	0.400	16	8	8	3	10
42	1/7/1972	ATL	W (+44)	39	5	7	0.714	4	4	1.000	14	3	8	2	14

G	Date	Opp	W/L	MP	FG	FGA	FG%	FT	FTA	FT%	TRB	AST	BLK	PF	PTS
43	1/9/1972	MIL	L (-16)	48	7	11	0.636	1	3	0.333	12	2	6	4	15
44	1/11/1972	DET	W (+20)	42	13	17	0.765	3	4	0.750	18	5		0	29
45	1/12/1972	CIN	L (-1)	46	8	14	0.571	8	14	0.571	19	4		2	24
46	1/14/1972	PHI	W (+14)	45	8	12	0.667	7	14	0.500	20	2	6	3	23
47	1/21/1972	NYK	L (-3)	45	12	16	0.750	4	12	0.333	19	2		3	28
48	1/22/1972	PHO	L (-14)	46	8	16	0.500	1	8	0.125	20	5		2	17
49	1/25/1972	PHO	W (+10)	42	4	7	0.571	8	17	0.471	18	5		3	16
50	1/28/1972	HOU	W (+13)	42	4	6	0.667	5	7	0.714	18	3		4	13
51	1/30/1972	POR	W (+22)	41	12	16	0.750	3	6	0.500	24	5		0	27
52	2/4/1972	MIL	W (+13)	48	8	14	0.571	2	8	0.250	25	3		2	18
53	2/5/1972	GSW	W (+12)	44	2	2	1.000	1	3	0.333	22	4		2	5
54	2/6/1972	BAL	W (+24)	29	6	6	1.000	5	11	0.455	12	2		2	17
55	2/8/1972	NYK	W (+5)	48	4	7	0.571	3	5	0.600	20	3		3	11
56	2/9/1972	ATL	W (+4)	48	8	12	0.667	3	3	1.000	10	1		1	19
57	2/11/1972	BOS	L (-13)	39	5	15	0.333	6	8	0.750	9	2		1	16
58	2/13/1972	BAL	W (+11)		8			1	3	0.333					17
59	2/15/1972	CIN	W (+7)	39	4	5	0.800	4	4	1.000	19	6		2	12
60	2/16/1972	PHO	L (-1)	48	6	10	0.600	7	12	0.583	21	5		4	19
61	2/18/1972	POR	W (+11)	35	9	9	1.000	1	6	0.167	14	2		1	19
62	2/19/1972	POR	W (+21)	38	4	7	0.571	5	8	0.625	19	8		2	13
63	2/20/1972	BOS	W (+19)	41	5	7	0.714	1	1	1.000	30	8		2	11

G	Date	Opp	W/L	MP	FG	FGA	FG%	FT	FTA	FT%	TRB	AST	BLK	PF	PTS
64	2/22/1972	DET	L (-1)	47	14	18	0.778	2	7	0.286	21	5		3	30
65	2/23/1972	HOU	L (-5)	46	1	7	0.143	8	13	0.615	14	3		1	10
66	2/25/1972	CIN	W (+21)	38	5	7	0.714	2	8	0.250	14	6		3	12
67	2/27/1972	CHI	W (+5)	53	7	8	0.875	1	8	0.125	23	3		4	15
68	2/29/1972	NYK	W (+3)	46	10	13	0.769	0	4	0.000	19	1		3	20
69	3/1/1972	MIL	W (+1)	48	3	5	0.600	2	6	0.333	17	5		4	8
70	3/3/1972	ATL	W (+10)	43	3	5	0.600	2	5	0.400	15	7		3	8
71	3/5/1972	BAL	L (-14)	41	4	4	1.000	2	3	0.667	14	3		2	10
72	3/7/1972	PHI	W (+17)	42	8	12	0.667	4	4	1.000	18	4		2	20
73	3/10/1972	CLE	W (+34)	40	8	11	0.727	3	8	0.375	18	3		2	19
74	3/12/1972	BUF	W (+39)	27	5	5	1.000	1	3	0.333	17	3	5	2	11
75	3/14/1972	DET	W (+13)	45	10	21	0.476	8	15	0.533	14	4		1	28
76	3/15/1972	CIN	W (+5)	48	7	12	0.583	3	5	0.600	24	1		3	17
77	3/17/1972	MIL	W (+16)	47	7	15	0.467	4	11	0.364	24	5		2	18
78	3/19/1972	GSW	W (+63)	25	5	6	0.833	0	1	0.000	10	6		2	10
79	3/21/1972	CHI	W (+5)	45	5	11	0.455	1	2	0.500	29	4		3	11
80	3/22/1972	CLE	L (-4)	48	10	17	0.588	3	9	0.333	19	5		4	23
81	3/24/1972	PHO	W (+2)	43	4	7	0.571	4	12	0.333	19	3		0	12
82	3/26/1972	SEA	W (+26)	37	3	4	0.750	1	2	0.500	23	5		3	7

1972 Playoffs

G	Date	Opp	W/L	MP	FG	FGA	FG%	FT	FTA	FT%	TRB	AST	BLK	PF	PTS
1	3/28/1972	CHI	W (+15)	48	3	3	1.000	4	8	0.599	17	6		0	10
2	3/30/1972	CHI	W (+7)	48	9	14	0.643	6	9	0.667	21	2		2	24
3	4/2/1972	CHI	W (+7)	48	6	12	0.500	4	6	0.667	14	0	9	5	16
4	4/4/1972	CHI	W (+11)	48	4	6	0.667	0	3	0.000	31	8		4	8
5	4/9/1972	MIL	L (-21)	43	3	12	0.250	4	16	0.250	24	0		3	10
6	4/12/1972	MIL	W (+1)	48	3	5	0.600	5	13	0.385	17	4		3	11
7	4/14/1972	MIL	W (+3)	47	1	3	0.333	5	9	0.556	14	4	10	4	7
8	4/16/1972	MIL	L (-26)	44	2	7	0.286	1	8	0.125	11	4	3	3	5
9	4/18/1972	MIL	W (+25)	45	2	3	0.667	8	8	1.000	26	6		2	12
10	4/22/1972	MIL	W (+4)	48	8	12	0.667	4	7	0.571	24	2	9	3	20
11	4/26/1972	NYK	L (-22)	40	5	11	0.455	2	3	0.667	19	1		4	12
12	4/30/1972	NYK	W (+14)	48	10	19	0.526	3	7	0.429	24	4		3	23
13	5/3/1972	NYK	W (+11)	48	9	10	0.900	8	11	0.727	20	1		4	26
14	5/5/1972	NYK	W (+5)	53	5	11	0.455	2	5	0.400	24	3	2+	5	12
15	5/7/1972	NYK	W (+14)	47	10	14	0.714	4	9	0.444	29	4	6	2	24

G	Date	Opp	W/L	MP	FG	FGA	FG%	FT	FTA	FT%	TRB	AST	BLK	PF	PTS
1	10/11/1972	KCO	W (+35)	32	3	3	1.000	1	9	0.111	13	4		1	7
2	10/13/1972	BOS	L (-8)	44	6	9	0.667	3	7	0.429	12	1		3	15
3	10/14/1972	NYK	L (-25)	38	7	10	0.700	2	3	0.667	14	5		4	16
4	10/15/1972	CLE	W (+12)	39	2	4	0.500	2	5	0.400	15	3	2	2	6
5	10/20/1972	POR	W (+22)	35	6	6	1.000	2	5	0.400	15	2	9	3	14
6	10/22/1972	CHI	W (+5)	44	6	8	0.750	1	4	0.250	22	1	12	0	13
7	10/24/1972	KCO	W (+20)		6	6	1.000	3	3	1.000	19	1		2	15
8	10/25/1972	HOU	W (+5)		10	12	0.833	1	5	0.200	20				21
9	10/27/1972	GSW	L (-28)	40	3	4	0.750	1	6	0.167	16	1	1	2	7
10	10/29/1972	PHO	W (+10)	45	6	7	0.857	0	2	0.000	21	9		1	12
11	11/3/1972	DET	W (+9)	45	10	12	0.833	2	8	0.250	19	1	7	3	22
12	11/4/1972	POR	W (+14)	45	8	11	0.727	2	8	0.250	18	4	7	1	18
13	11/5/1972	SEA	W (+9)	43	9	11	0.818	6	12	0.500	9	1		3	24
14	11/7/1972	HOU	W (+13)	39	5	7	0.714	1	2	0.500	19	6		1	11
15	11/10/1972	CLE	W (+30)	32	5	5	1.000	1	1	1.000	16	5	8	0	11
16	11/14/1972	MIL	W (+3)	44	8	12	0.667	0	2	0.000	15	1		2	16
17	11/15/1972	DET	W (+11)	42	9	10	0.900	3	3	1.000	21	4			21
18	11/17/1972	BUF	W (+3)	43	6	6	1.000	1	4	0.250	16	3		2	13
19	11/19/1972	PHI	W (+40)	27	6	8	0.750	2	2	1.000	13	3		0	14
20	11/24/1972	DET	W (+17)	31	7	8	0.875	0	0	1.000	9	5		1	14
21	11/25/1972	PHO	W (+7)	44	5	7	0.714	8	12	0.667	20	12			18

G	Date	Opp	W/L	MP	FG	FGA	FG%	FT	FTA	FT%	TRB	AST	BLK	PF	PTS
22	11/26/1972	PHO	W (+5)	44	9	11	0.818	2	8	0.250	26	1		3	20
23	12/1/1972	ATL	L (-5)	49	2	3	0.667	3	4	0.750	24	3		5	7
24	12/2/1972	GSW	W (+9)		1	3	0.333	4	4	1.000	17			3	6
25	12/5/1972	MIL	W (+22)	43	4	4	1.000	1	2	0.500	15	7		4	9
26	12/8/1972	SEA	W (+19)	39	1	1	1.000	1	1	1.000	16	7		2	3
27	12/10/1972	POR	W (+36)	35	5	5	1.000	4	5	0.800	17	5		3	14
28	12/12/1972	CHI	W (+1)	48	3	5	0.600	2	3	0.667	23	3		2	8
29	12/13/1972	PHI	W (+38)	35	3	3	1.000	8	13	0.615	15	2	15	1	14
30	12/15/1972	BOS	L (-4)	44	6	10	0.600	6	16	0.375	14	1		2	18
31	12/19/1972	BUF	W (+26)	44	10	14	0.714	5	7	0.714	22	7			25
32	12/20/1972	BAL	W (+6)	46	7	8	0.875	1	3	0.333	20	1			15
33	12/22/1972	PHO	L (-8)	48	2	4	0.500	1	10	0.100	23	6		2	5
34	12/26/1972	POR	W (+24)	39	3	4	0.750	5	7	0.714	16	2		4	11
35	12/27/1972	HOU	L (-32)	48	5			2	2	1.000	20	4			12
36	12/29/1972	KCO	W (+29)	40	4	6	0.667	2	4	0.500	26	5	7	0	10
37	1/1/1973	SEA	W (+5)		3			0	0		20	5			6
38	1/2/1973	GSW	L (-6)	48	1	1	1.000	0	0		21	5		4	2
39	1/6/1973	CLE	L (-15)		2			2	3	0.667	15				6
40	1/7/1973	MIL	L (-7)	48	3	5	0.600	3	6	0.500	18	2		3	9
41	1/10/1973	PHI	W (+24)	36	2	2	1.000	5	8	0.625	14	4		0	9
42	1/12/1973	CHI	W (+12)	48	2	7	0.286	3	5	0.600	24	4		4	7

G	Date	Opp	W/L	MP	FG	FGA	FG%	FT	FTA	FT%	TRB	AST	BLK	PF	PTS
43	1/14/1973	ATL	W (+2)		3	5	0.600	3	7	0.429	14				9
44	1/16/1973	BAL	L (-8)	46	7	7	1.000	2	5	0.400	26	2			16
45	1/19/1973	NYK	W (+7)	48	1	3	0.333	0	4	0.000	24	4		2	2
46	1/20/1973	PHO	W (+20)	38	3	8	0.375	4	5	0.800	11	4			10
47	1/21/1973	KCO	W (+21)	43	9	11	0.818	11	19	0.579	21	6		2	29
48	1/26/1973	GSW	W (+16)	44	3	3	1.000	0	2	0.000	17	1		2	6
49	1/27/1973	GSW	W (+15)	42	4	5	0.800	3	7	0.429	14	4		3	11
50	1/28/1973	SEA	W (+36)	38	8	10	0.800	6	16	0.375	19	9	7	2	22
51	1/30/1973	CHI	W (+3)	48	4	6	0.667	4	12	0.333	18	3		4	12
52	2/1/1973	PHO	W (+14)	45	8	12	0.667	9	11	0.818	19	8		2	25
53	2/2/1973	HOU	W (+17)	44	5	8	0.625	8	11	0.727	21	3		3	18
54	2/4/1973	BAL	W (+10)	46	2	6	0.333	5	6	0.833	20	8			9
55	2/6/1973	NYK	W (+5)	48	2	6	0.333	1	6	0.167	24	3	7	2	5
56	2/7/1973	BOS	L (-1)	48	4	7	0.571	5	7	0.714	19	3		4	13
57	2/9/1973	MIL	L (-21)	44	3	3	1.000	2	2	1.000	14	4		2	8
58	2/11/1973	PHI	W (+18)	46	5	8	0.625	2	5	0.400	31	5		2	12
59	2/13/1973	SEA	W (+3)	48	7	8	0.875	4	8	0.500	18	5		3	18
60	2/16/1973	BAL	W (+18)	36	4	5	0.800	3	5	0.600	17	3		0	11
61	2/17/1973	POR	W (+7)	48	6	9	0.667	5	10	0.500	31	11	6	2	17
62	2/18/1973	ATL	L (-7)	48	5	8	0.625	0	3	0.000	21	4		2	10
63	2/20/1973	CHI	L (-14)	40	5	9	0.556	6	9	0.667	24	1		3	16

G	Date	Opp	W/L	MP	FG	FGA	FG%	FT	FTA	FT%	TRB	AST	BLK	PF	PTS
64	2/21/1973	DET	L (-8)		9	17	0.529	0	0		19				18
65	2/23/1973	GSW	L (-5)	48	1	2	0.500	2	3	0.667	15	7	10	2	4
66	2/25/1973	MIL	W (+9)	46	10	14	0.714	4	5	0.800	20	4		3	24
67	2/27/1973	KCO	L (-4)	43	4	8	0.500	4	8	0.500	19	4		5	12
68	3/2/1973	CHI	W (+20)	40	4	5	0.800	5	7	0.714	26	7		3	13
69	3/4/1973	CLE	W (+43)	40	2	3	0.667	0	0		13	7	8	3	4
70	3/6/1973	POR	W (+12)	48	9	12	0.750	4	8	0.500	24	5	7	1	22
71	3/9/1973	BOS	L (-8)	48	4	8	0.500	3	4	0.750	13	4		3	11
72	3/11/1973	DET	W (+24)	39	11	15	0.733	0	1	0.000	14	5		1	22
73	3/13/1973	BUF	W (+9)		10	12	0.833	5	7	0.714	23				25
74	3/14/1973	DET	W (+9)	48	9	10	0.900	4	4	1.000	13	2		3	22
75	3/16/1973	NYK	L (-11)	48	6	8	0.750	2	8	0.250	22	2		1	14
76	3/18/1973	PHO	W (+18)	48	7	8	0.875	2	3	0.667	15	8		3	16
77	3/20/1973	ATL	L (-2)		6	11	0.545	1	2	0.500	23	3			13
78	3/21/1973	KCO	W (+6)		8	9	0.889	3	4	0.750	20	7		2	19
79	3/23/1973	BUF	W (+20)	44	8	8	1.000	3	7	0.429	24	7		4	19
80	3/25/1973	SEA	W (+16)		8	8	1.000	4	6	0.667	20	3			20
81	3/27/1973	MIL	L (-1)	46	0	0		0	0		14	4		2	0
82	3/28/1973	GSW	W (+7)	48	0	1	0.000	1	2	0.500	18	9		0	1

1973 Playoffs

G	Date	Opp	W/L	MP	FG	FGA	FG%	FT	FTA	FT%	TRB	AST	BLK	PF	PTS
1	3/30/1973	CHI	W (+3)	53	3	5	0.600	5	10	0.500	20	2		2	11
2	4/1/1973	CHI	W (+15)	48	2	5	0.400	0	2	0.000	21	5	11	2	4
3	4/6/1973	CHI	L (-10)	44	1	6	0.167	0	0		18	3		3	2
4	4/8/1973	CHI	L (-4)	47	3	7	0.429	5	7	0.714	30	0	12	4	11
5	4/10/1973	CHI	W (+21)	48	8	11	0.727	5	12	0.417	29	4		4	21
6	4/13/1973	CHI	L (-8)	48	4	5	0.800	6	10	0.600	26	4		4	14
7	4/15/1973	CHI	W (+3)	48	10	17	0.588	1	1	1.000	28	4	8	2	21
8	4/17/1973	GSW	W (+2)	44	2	5	0.400	0	0		25	2	8	4	4
9	4/19/1973	GSW	W (+11)	48	1	3	0.333	3	4	0.750	30	4		0	5
10	4/21/1973	GSW	W (+56)	39	2	2	1.000	8	10	0.800	25	3		2	12
11	4/23/1973	GSW	L (-8)	48	4	6	0.667	1	1	1.000	16	3		2	9
12	4/25/1973	GSW	W (+10)	46	2	2	1.000	1	3	0.333	22	7		3	5
13	5/1/1973	NYK	W (+3)	48	5	11	0.455	2	4	0.500	20	6	7	3	12
14	5/3/1973	NYK	L (-4)	48	2	4	0.500	1	9	0.111	20	0		3	5
15	5/6/1973	NYK	L (-4)	48	2	3	0.667	1	4	0.250	13	5		4	5
16	5/8/1973	NYK	L (-5)	48	4	8	0.500	5	7	0.714	19	5		3	13
17	5/10/1973	NYK	L (-9)	48	9	16	0.563	5	14	0.357	21	3	2	3	23

9. POST SCRIPT

Something that has occurred to me during my years of watching professional basketball – and I believe it is true for other sports as well – is that players often speak as they play.

For example, in conversation Wilt was always good-natured and amiable, but always had very definite points of view that he wanted to get across. He filled his speech with smiles and chuckles, filling awkward pauses with friendly, self-deprecating interjections – but his points were made in an overpowering fashion. He controlled a conversation like he controlled a basketball court, by covering all the angles and by concluding his sentences with a slam dunk or a blocked shot.

Bill Russell has a different style of speaking in much the same way that his game was different. He often begins a sentence slowly, as if he has no idea what he is going to say, but then sneaks up on you and finally bursts forth with a startling insight that leaves the interviewer speechless. He then raises his brow as if to say almost exactly what he says about his shot blocking: "Yes, I did that to you. And if you ask me another question, I'll do it to you again!"

Kareem Abdul-Jabbar also seems to talk as he played. He's more soft-spoken than Wilt was; more reserved – but just as opinionated. His replies to questions are deliberate, eloquent, and methodical – just like his preparation for the sky hook – and his conclusions are usually just as undeniable.

Wavering Knots